Presenting

HOLLYWOOD ALBUM

Melvyn Douglas, Cary Grant and Myrna Loy.

Alexis Smith.

HOLLYWOOD

in the 1940s

THE STARS' OWN STORIES

EDITED BY IVY CRANE WILSON / FOREWORD BY LIZ SMITH

FREDERICK UNGAR PUBLISHING CO. / NEW YORK

CONTENTS

		Page
FOREWORD	*Liz Smith*	7
STARS AND THEIR FAMILIES		10
INTRODUCING THE ALBUM	*Ivy Crane Wilson*	12
HORSES ARE MY HOBBY	*Ronald Reagan*	13
SHOP TALK OF THE STUDIOS	*Ray Milland*	16
MY MOST IMPORTANT ROLE	*Maureen O'Hara*	21
HOLD THAT LINE!	*Edith Head*	25
WHAT MAKES A GOOD WESTERN . . .	*Rod Cameron*	28
THE SANTANA AND I	*Humphrey Bogart*	33
THE GENIE OF ALADDIN'S LAMP WORKED FOR ME .	*Evelyn Keyes*	39
THE STORY OF A GREAT STUDIO . . .	*David Hanna*	43
ALL MY FRIENDS ARE NEIGHBOURS TO ME . .	*Shirley Temple Agar*	46
CHARLIE McCARTHY AND EDGAR BERGEN DISCUSS TELEVISION		49
I AM A ROLLING STONE	*Burt Lancaster*	51
THE WESTMORE SAGA	*Perc Westmore*	57
FOR YOU—NEW FACES	*Michael Curtiz*	61
AROUND THE WORLD TO HOLLYWOOD . .	*Peter Lawford*	64
IT'S DRAMA, NOT GLAMOUR, FOR ME! . .	*Ann Blyth*	68
I'M AN ARTIST—BY ACCIDENT	*Mel Archer*	71
HOLLYWOOD FASHION PARADE		74

CONTENTS

		Page
STARS OFF DUTY		83
VARIETY IS THE SPICE OF MY LIFE	*Loretta Young*	91
JUST AN INVENTOR AT HEART	*Alan Hale*	95
ANSWERS INC.	*Irene Dunne*	99
GET IN THERE AND SWIM !	*Johnny Weissmuller*	102
I DRESSED A QUEEN	*Leah Rhodes*	104
CLARK GABLE LIKES TO ROAM . . . WITH THE DESTINATION UNKNOWN		109
MUSIC IS THE MOTHER OF FANTASY	*Walt Disney*	113
MY DAUGHTERS AND I	*Joan Bennett*	116
GET THAT PROP	*" Limey " Plews*	120
SPECTACULAR BOSS	*Faith Domergue*	122
INGRID BERGMAN HAD A DREAM	*Victor Fleming*	127
THOUGHTS FROM A HILLTOP	*Lew Ayres*	131
UP IN THE AIR	*Gene Raymond*	134
CALIFORNIA GARDENS ARE LOVELY	*Greer Garson*	137
I WAS STAKED TO A CAREER	*Dana Andrews*	140
THANKS TO MY DANCING	*Betty Grable*	145
CHOOSING THE WORLD'S MOST BEAUTIFUL GIRLS	*Earl Carroll*	148
FILMS OF THE FUTURE		152
MEET MY CHILDREN	*Joan Crawford*	154
OUT OF THE HAT	*Peter Godfrey*	157

Foreword

I BELIEVE that when an irresistible force of time meets an immovable object like a place—the moment can be historically and sentimentally very special. Certainly one of the most recent special times had to have been a head-trip known as Hollywood in the Forties. In reality, which has nothing to do with Hollywood, the first half of the decade placed all able-bodied men in uniform and basic training. Older flat-footed fellows could join the Civil Air Patrol and warn their neighbors to black out the windows against air raids that thankfully never happened. Women wore colorful crocheted hairnets called snoods to their new factory jobs. Trousers called slacks hid the fact that nylons had gone to war, along with rubber, gasoline, red meat, and sugar.

Kids flattened tin cans and rolled tinfoil into massive balls for the "war effort." You either sold or bought Girl Scout cookies. Gals and *guys* were most likely virgins until married, and you were the object of pity and derision if your parents were divorced. On June evenings New York's Central Park played host to the fireflies, and I don't mean a rock group or street gang of the same name, but honest-to-goodness lightning bugs. Honesty and goodness were as ubiquitous as the motion picture house around which every prairie tank-town and metropolitan borough was centered. Movies ran continuous double features, short subjects, newsreels, and cartoons. On Saturday, there were serials to-be-continued.

When you weren't at the movies, you read about the stars in countless fan magazines like "Modern Screen." Teenagers taped quarters to mail order forms and got back autographed photos of their favorite stars. Ronald Reagan and Lon McAllister were pinned next to my high school pennant above my dresser. Hollywood in the Forties was not merely a place, but a fantasy called love—and its magic spell was everywhere.

Hollywood in the Thirties had been extravagant, moderne, brittle, top hat and white fox, scandalously sophisticated, and outrageously profitable for the studios. The rest of the country was spreading pork fat instead of butter on its Wonder bread, but movie stars banked virtually untaxed salaries, played tennis, drove Rolls-Royces, and sailed for Europe on luxury liners between marriages. The silverscreen's queen, Joan Crawford, ran off with the prince of Pickfair, Douglas Fairbanks, Jr., against family (his) and studio (hers) wishes. When she later divorced Fairbanks to marry Franchot Tone, Hollywood hardly commented except to cluck that Crawford had always been a social climber.

But with the arrival of the Forties such candor became unfashionable. Posters bore warnings that "A slip of the lip, can sink a ship." Personal anonymity disappeared with the draft. Anyone with a high profile was fair game for gossip columnists like Louella, Hedda, Kilgallen, and Winchell, who behaved like reigning terrorists by holding public executions daily in syndicated print. Control was the keynote of the decade, whether it was the government witch-hunting communists or studio rajah Louis B. Mayer boycotting his actors so that they could not work.

World War II put away the Great Depression, but the international marketplace also disappeared. Hollywood was hurting. Stars were forced to take salary cuts, and had little to say about what terrible films they made. Only Bette Davis was untouchable and nervy enough to stand up to the brothers Warner, whose studio was called "the penitentiary" by insiders. Of course, swashbuckler Errol Flynn continued to make headlines and underage girls; and drive a car bearing the license plate "R U 18." The indomitable Katharine Hepburn was quoted as saying: "I don't care what they print, as long as it *isn't* true." But the industry was tightening its grip and its belt as profits shrunk. Hollywood in the Forties began in black and white, and was lean all over.

Low budgets also reduced production costs. Backgrounds became mere shadows, and the shadows became a presence, especially in the expert hands of German and Austrian expatriates Lang, Wilder, Zinnemann, and the Hungarian Michael Curtiz. Cameramen like James Wong Howe, Lee Garmes, and Lucien Ballard became penultimate powers, and a *genre* was born that the French would later call *cinéma noir*. The men, Cotten, Heflin, Ladd, and the immortal Bogart, wore fedoras, trenchcoats, and a mien of desperation. The women, Stanwyck, Astor, Davis, and *siempre* Crawford, wore mink. Sneers strained their fabulous faces, and deep in the fur's folds a beautifully manicured hand gripped a revolver, which proved the *femme fatal*. My favorite of the "black" period are "The Unsuspected," "Dark Passage," "The Maltese Falcon," "Woman in the Window," "Sorry, Wrong Number," and the song "Tangerine" playing on an unseen radio in "Double Indemnity."

The Great War inspired a white-washing of American grassroots that would take more than a decade of Fifties' conservatism and Freudian analysis to paint over. Apple pie, Momism, Andy Hardy, and white picket fences replaced the grapes of wrath and the social reformers of the Thirties. Abject poverty was unpatriotic, though genteel poverty flourished as honorable. Outside Hollywood the world was bombing itself to smithereens, but back home in Indiana, musicals were put on in the barn; priests crooned you into going their way, and only the Westerns grew florid and suggestively sexy. The story of "Duel in the Sun," with Jennifer Jones in her grand state of *déshabillé*, might stand today as a libretto for grand opera.

The studios divided up the spoils and specialized. M.G.M. had the most and the biggest stars: Mickey Rooney, Gable, Greer Garson, Tracy, Gene Kelly, and directors Stanley Donen and Vincente Minnelli. M.G.M.'s movies were like Hallmark greeting cards with bluebirds and ivy framing nice people who had ideals even when heartbroken, and quite naturally burst into song at the drop of a music cue. Warner Brothers locked up the melodramas, biographies, and the "black" films with an iron-fisted tenacity that paid off handsomely. At Paramount, comedies, farce, and costumed period pieces held sway. Columbia boasted Rita Hayworth in "Gilda," and mountains of *kitsch*. 20th Century-Fox had Betty Grable to pin-up on every soldier's locker. Universal offered Deanna Durbin, Maria Montez and Sabu. R.K.O. and Eagle Lion ground out B-pictures by the mile, while Republic had Vera Hruba Ralston. Disney gave us Mickey Mouse and "Fantasia." And they all made war films.

Stars such as Gable, James Stewart, Tyrone Power, and Doug Fairbanks pinned on officers' bars and went to war. The women stayed home, served endless coffee and doughnuts, and danced democratically with the enlisted men at U.S.O. canteens. The Andrews Sisters sang on and on about bugle boys and rum and Coca-Cola. Hollywood in the Forties had no reality, and no one was allowed to puncture our perfect state of naïveté. We saw, we read, we believed.

Ronald Reagan loved his horses, and the thought that one day he might be elected Governor of

California or run for President as a conservative Republican was ludicrous. Joan Crawford loved her children to distraction. That thirty years later her oldest, Christina, would write an auto-biographical exposé, "Mommie Dearest," portraying her mother as cruel and abusive, was, and to some, still is, sacrilege. No one would have guessed that Shirley Temple and John Agar would ever divorce. But then none of us back then could imagine that their marriage had been a scheme of the studio's to save Shirley's flagging career. Alan Ladd was tough, silent, and sexy. We never knew he was but five feet four, let alone that his serious drinking bouts led to attempted suicides with final success. Who could have known, and who would have printed that while Evelyn Keyes was married to John Huston in ballyhooed bliss, she once jerked a smooching blonde off Huston's lap in her own home and said, pointing to Enrica Soma, Huston's future wife, "That's his mistress, I'm his wife, and *you* are one too many." No one remembers that the brilliant actor Lew Ayres appeared in a total of fifty-three films by 1942, but after he declared himself a conscientious objector during the war, he made but three more movies that decade, one of which was the lovely "Johnny Belinda." Looking back, it is all *déjà-vu*: an animated cliché in Technicolor.

Looking back, I can only smile, which is what this book will make you do. Somehow I think it was better not knowing all the inside dope—the awful truth—that Watergate and the subsequent Seventies dumped on us. The apple pies of yesterday have crumbled into today's Twinkies. Musicals are no longer sentimental, but shocking biographies of personal decadence like "The Rose," and "All That Jazz." Yet some part of me remains loyal to those fantasy years. I'm happy in the knowledge that Hollywood really doesn't change. Today, I'm a "powerful" columnist so I don't have to send quarters for photos of my favorite stars. Above my desk is still pinned a picture of Robert Redford standing next to his ultimate fan—me. Forty years later, Hollywood is still Olympus inhabited by gods: a special place in a special time warp of its own.

LIZ SMITH

Stars and their

Bruce Bennett is obviously very proud of his young son.

Bill Holden and his attractive star wife, Brenda Marshall, watch Virginia, aged 10, West, aged 3, and the baby Scotty, aged 14 months, at play in the pool at their home.

One of the biggest families in Hollywood belongs to Maureen O'Sullivan, wife of Director John Farrow. Since this picture there has been a fifth newcomer!

Mr. and Mrs. Wayne Morris relax with their little daughter, who is named Pam.

Families

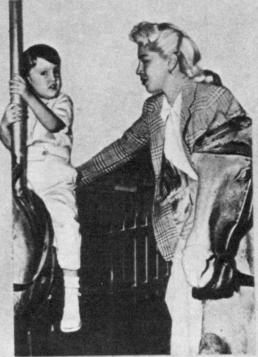

Paul Henreid, romantic star of the screen, is caught by the candid camera at home with his wife and two blonde youngsters, Mimi and Monica.

Dennis Morgan and his three fine youngsters enjoy themselves in the water. Mother's staying out, but Stanley, Kristin and little James are loving it !

The Carousal is still a favourite carnival ride for Cheryl and her mother, Lana Turner.

Four year old Alana Ladd is the centre of interest inside the caravan where Alan Ladd lived during the filming of Paramount's forthcoming " Whispering Smith."

INTRODUCING *the* ALBUM

HOLLYWOOD ALBUM brings you stories from stars, producers, directors and others whose lives are identified with Hollywood. This collection of views, news, and behind-the-scenes tales is given in an informal style to enable those interested to get an inside glimpse of what goes on in the studios and film circles.

In this Album you will notice stories by several new stars, including Burt Lancaster, Ann Blyth, and Faith Domergue, the last named a Howard Hughes discovery. Readers who admire the long-time favourites will notice stories written by Irene Dunne, Clark Gable, Joan Bennett and Greer Garson. Shirley Temple has the rather unique position of being both an old and a young star. She started to write her story before she went to the hospital for the birth of her baby, Linda Susan, and finished it shortly after the baby was born. Shirley and her handsome husband, John Agar, last year made their first picture together, "Fort Apache."

There is so much to be told about Hollywood life, it is hard to get it all between the covers of one book. We have tried to give you as much variety as possible. If we have overlooked your pet subject or you do not find your favourite star represented among the contributors, perhaps you will find them in next year's Album.

Bob Hope had a busy year with his work in pictures and the demands made on him to tour the country for various charity drives, but we managed to get his summing up of Hollywood as given in "The Hollywood Reporter" survey: "Hollywood is a funny place where a comedian can go about his business of bringing a smile to the world, and still lead a normal life with family and friends; where gorgeous glamour girls of the screen are real life wives who get a big kick out of diaper shopping for the baby; where Bing Crosby joins millions of other Americans as a 'grandstand expert' in enjoying our great national pastime of baseball. Hollywood is churches, homes, stores, movie houses, dull people, interesting people and, yes, swimming pools. To those of us who really know Hollywood—and are proud to call it home—it really isn't so 'different.' If you should have occasion to ask me, I'd say it's pretty solid stuff."

Everyone has his or her own opinion of Hollywood, but it might prove of interest that, according to a recent survey, only eleven per cent of those employed in the film industry are women, in spite of the emphasis given feminine beauty. The majority of top stars are in their forties. The divorce rate among film stars is a trifle lower than that of the rest of the nation. Eighty per cent of the Hollywood people believe that the world, through its newspapers and magazines, gets an incorrect impression of life in the film industry. Fifteen per cent of film stars are teetotalers. Thirty per cent do not smoke, and forty per cent do not go to nightclubs.

But, regardless of facts and figures, whether stars drive sleek, specially designed motor cars or yellow jeeps, bathe in gold-tapped bathtubs or ordinary showers, live in palatial mansions or rented apartments, their common cause is to entertain audiences around the world with romance, comedy, tragedy and excitement.

In "Hollywood Album" they give us a glimpse of the real behind the make-believe.

HORSES are my

SOMEONE once said that every man should have a hobby which involved a certain amount of physical risk. If this is correct, then I have been fortunate enough to find such a hobby—as a long list of wine purchases will bear witness. Briefly, the hobby is horses. The wine enters the picture because of an old cavalry tradition that when one dismounts at the horse's suggestion, a bottle of champagne must be furnished by the deposed rider.

Perhaps, however, this is too abrupt an opening for a discussion of the hobby which threatens to supersede pictures in my thoughts and every day life. Many years ago I found myself with an irresistible and unaccountable desire to ride a horse. I say " unaccountable " because I was not raised in the country ; I had no experience with horses ; in fact, had never been on one. I made the usual livery stable start with a hired horse and makeshift habit until a friend introduced me to the military programme of the Cavalry Reserve. By enlisting as a candidate for a commission, army mounts automatically became available, plus instruction by regular army officers. Even so, riding was a weekend sport and many times an intermittent one—until I came to Hollywood. And here I must confess that my hobby became very much sidetracked. I was in a new job—in virtually a new world—and, also, here in California most riding follows the western

HOBBY

says RONALD REAGAN

Ronald Reagan's greatest hobby is horse-riding, and his enthusiasm is shared by Nino Pepitone, his riding instructor and partner.

tradition, meaning western saddles—stock saddles—and horses trained as cow ponies. I am frank to say this type of riding couldn't hold my interest.

Then came a war and, with the usual military efficiency, I, a cavalry officer, found myself assigned to the Air Corps. When the war ended I had spent four years collecting dust on my boots, with no sound or sight of a horse. But by some Hollywood miracle, my first picture following release from service was called " Stallion Road " and was the story of a young doctor of animals who also raised and trained thoroughbred hunters. I can't really say that I worried much about the story content. I gave the studio my O.K. when, on page 65, I discovered a scene in which I jumped a horse. Naturally, there was a certain difficulty to overcome : namely, the studio's tendency to use a double for any scene involving physical action. But I was determined that this scene I would do myself and offered as a lure to Warner's the idea of setting the camera at such an angle that it would be apparent to the audience that I was doing the jumping. Upon winning this fight I suddenly remembered four horseless years, and decided a little brushing up might come in handy.

Again a Hollywood miracle introduced me to a gentleman, Nino Pepitone. Nino is a free lance actor—in fact, you might see him as the French head waiter in " Voice of the Turtle "—but my introduction was not on the basis of acting. Nino is a former officer in the Royal Italian Cavalry, a graduate of Pinirollo . . . to the horseman this needs no explanation, for the Italian Cavalry has long been known as the father of all modern horsemanship and armies all over the world have for many years sent their top cavalry officers to Italy to study equitation.

A third miracle, Hollywood variety, happened, for my script called for a black thoroughbred mare. My first coaching session with Nino was on a black thoroughbred mare which he owned and had trained as a hunter. So Nino ended up with " Stallion Road " and so did the black mare—Tar Baby. By the time the picture had ended, Tar Baby was mine and Nino and I were partners in a horse-breeding establishment now known as "Yearling Row." I might add we are in business as an excuse to pursue our hobby.

But there is more to it than this. We share a theory—a theory that to many breeders of thoroughbreds, who have gone in for quantity and have ignored the benefits to be derived from personal handling of brood mares and foals, seems unworkable. Naturally it is too early to claim proof of our theory, but all of our brood mares are trained as hunters ; all of them, even when in foal, are worked practically up to the time of foaling. When the foals are about three weeks old the mother goes back under saddle and the foal goes out on a lead, working by her side. Whether we ever produce a Derby winner or not, we will still challenge anyone to compare their brood mares, standing as most do, year in, year out in pasture, with our mares still able to clear fences while in foal.

This is the basic theory of "Yearling Row" as a business. Whether we ever become rich from it is beside the point. I don't know how to evaluate in dollars and cents the physical well-being, the mental stimulation and the all-round joy of living which has come to us from our thoroughbreds. We have tried to repay them by making kindness in our riding and training a set rule. In schooling for jumping we do not use a chute : we try to make jumping something the horse wants to do for pleasure. We use the Italian style forward seat saddles, and we ride the Italian, or forward seat, method. To explain why this is a kindness to the horse would be not a brief article on hobbies, but a very thick book in itself. Many people, completely kind-hearted, have no conception of the cruelty they unwittingly inflict on a horse by sitting back, their weight bouncing down on the horse's loins, and an unnecessarily heavy bit in the horse's mouth. I might add here that we use the lightest type of broken snaffle on all our horses, and even though some have been obtained from the race track and are somewhat unruly and excitable as a result, we still ride them with this mild bit ; and see no necessity for a mechanical contrivance aimed at stopping a horse by pain and pressure.

As a parent of two children, I only hope that I can instil in them a desire to participate in this sport. I feel they will be grateful for the companionship and joy which will always be theirs ; and I, as a parent, will know that they have learned self-reliance, unselfishness, the ability to think of self last, and the joy of doing —because our riding begins with grooming and saddling the horse, and ends with rubbing, blanketing and stabling—which, incidentally, makes for a full day and, I am afraid, a full article.

Ronald and Nino set off for the morning ride on the former's Californian ranch. They will both be appearing in Warner Bros. forthcoming " The Voice of the Turtle."

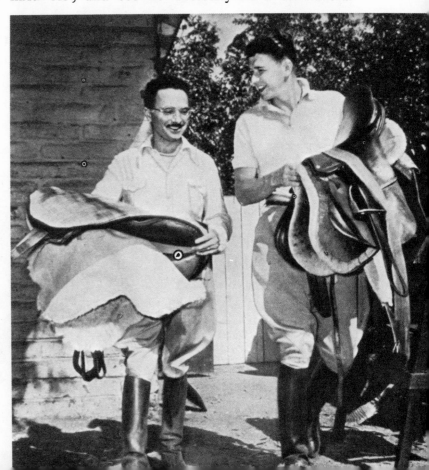

SHOP TALK OF THE STUDIOS

ACTUALLY there is very little discernible difference between Hollywood and Britain in the matter of picture-making—the stages look the same, even share a dank, somewhat musty odour; but there is one phase of the business that definitely would not be interchangeable: that is the terminology.

I became so interested in the difference that I began making a list which I will give you at the end of this article. It was very interesting to me to note just how much film people the world over have in common. One great common denominator is the same expression of harassment. It's a sort of occupation trade-mark. I am willing to bet that if you happened to stroll onto a motion picture set in Equatorial West Africa or Indo-China, you would find it there. The studio executives worry about whether or not the producer will bring in the picture within the prescribed time. The director worries about his players—that they will not become ill, over-temperamental, etc.; the actors worry over their parts; the rest of the crew worry on general principles; and not until the last day of shooting do we see people showing any real relaxation. Then everyone enjoys the traditional party given on the stage to mark the winding-up of the film. Many people think making pictures is just one big, beautiful game—all glamour and highly exciting. They forget that all concerned have to be up with the dawn and practically to bed with the sparrows. No parties, no fun, nothing but hard, gruelling work—so perhaps the harassed look is understandable.

From the progress that has been made in films—especially in British film production—I am quite sure there is no reason for the worried look. While I was playing at Denham in " So Evil My Love," in 1947, I was

Ray Milland and Ann Todd are teamed together in " So Evil My Love," a Paramount-British production.

keenly impressed with the general efficiency of all concerned. It was quite different from the pre-war days. It seems this new awareness was born during the war years when good pictures were turned out under the strain of constant air attack and a general disruption of all phases of life. In America, film companies were harassed by certain shortages in man-power and machinery, etc., but they never had the added strain of actual attack.

Nowadays there is little difference between the physical aspect of Hollywood and British film studios. The stages look the same, they are manned by the same size crews. One advantage Hollywood has is climatic conditions—no other place in the world seems so blessed with the right kind of weather as Hollywood. Every once in a while some other place threatens to make inroads on the film industry and establish studios away from Hollywood. It always fades into nothingness. New York makes periodic tries. There was quite a lot of talk of setting up rival studios just outside of Las Vegas in Nevada; Mexico City made its bid, and so it goes; but Hollywood goes on grinding out the biggest part of the world's supply of films.

Now that air transport has cut down travelling time, it makes it possible for actors and others engaged in film-making to work on both sides of the Atlantic and get a change of atmosphere. I think it is good for us all to exchange viewpoints. I even did a lot of commuting before the war, and only a chance meeting with Joe Egli, Paramount's casting director, led to my present contract with Paramount and more or less settled position.

My contract with Paramount started in 1934, but it has been a rather slow climb to that eventful night in 1946 when I was given an Oscar for playing that

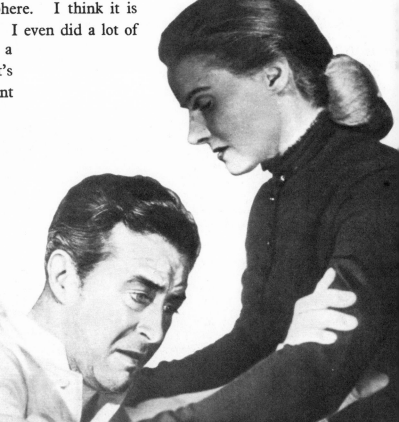

Ray came over to Denham to make "So Evil My Love" with British star Ann Todd.

17

disreputable fellow, Don Birnam, the dipsomaniac of "The Lost Weekend."

I was very glad to return to London to make "So Evil My Love"—it gave me a chance to show my wife and Danny, my young son, my favourite haunts around London. When they came to see me on the set I had to explain to them the difference in the naming of practically everything concerned with the making of the picture. Here is the list I got together to show the difference in terminology:

HOLLYWOOD		LONDON
On the stage	On the set	On the floor
Cameraman	Director of Cinematography	Lighting Director
Start	Get going	Get cracking
Member of camera crew	Assistant cameraman	Focus puller
Carpenters	Carpenters	Chippies
Platform	Parallel	Rostrum
Truck	Truck	Lorry
Anything on four wheels that moves	Car	Transport
It may be difficult	Impossible	You've had it !
Head electrician	Gaffer	Charge hand
Asst. head electrician	Best boy	Asst. charge hand
Future Corporation heads	Office boys	Nippers
„ „ „	Messengers	Runners
Performers	Actors	Artistes
Atmosphere players Extras		Crowd
General assistants on stage Grips		Stags
Hanging platform from which lights are suspended Scaffolds		Cradles
Small light Baby		Pup
Smaller light Peanut		Dinky
Familiar method of greeting to assistant directors You're nuts !		You're crackers !

The part that won Ray Milland the Oscar Award was Don Birnam in " Lost Weekend." Jane Wyman gave a very sincere performance opposite him.

MY MOST IMPORTANT ROLE by MAUREEN O'HARA

IT is a most satisfying and delightful experience to be rated a star, but being Mrs. Will Price is the all-important thing. Nothing can ever make up for a fine husband, a home filled with happy children and run in the old-fashioned way. By that I mean the husband is really the master of the house. I am frankly old-fashioned.

From the start of our marriage I asked that the telephone in our house be answered with " This is the Price residence "—and it always is ; I have been firm about that.

I do not depreciate any of the advantages that are mine as a result of my career and I am very happy when my name is in the first ten, as it was in a recent trade magazine poll, the Box Office Digest ; but I would give it all up if I thought it interfered with the happiness of my home and the well-being of my little daughter, Bronwyn. I am most fortunate in having an excellent nurse for her, Eleanor Blair. She has complete charge of her while I am away and I never dispute her discipline of Bronwyn ; but when I am home and in charge, she never interferes with my orders, so Bronwyn is never confused. She knows she cannot run from one to the other to get her own way.

After I get through the day's work at the studio I am careful to remove every trace of make-up, wear very simple clothes and come home to my family without any trace of the studio about me. I never discuss my part, the day's worries or triumphs, unless, of course, my husband specifically asks, which he seldom does. He is interested in my career, naturally, but at home there is so much to talk about of purely family interest, neither of us even thinks of talking of our careers. Will is a director at R.K.O. Radio Pictures and I think a very fine one, at least—that's what they tell me.

We are essentially simple people, which made much less pronounced the troubles so many had during the war in getting domestic help—gardeners, etc. Our house is large, and requires several servants to keep it in order. But when we saw the difficulties, we closed most of the house, keeping open only necessary rooms. If we were without servants I could and did clean my own house. My mother very sensibly insisted that we children —she has six—learn how to do everything pertaining to housework. I can remember being rebellious about it when there were flowers in the field for the picking and an anxious dog on the mat waiting to play, and I grumbled a little. In vain, though. Mother was adamant. Now I am so grateful to her. Housekeeping became a habit with me and it certainly pays off in peace of mind and a happy house. The servants, too, have more respect for a mistress who knows how to clean a bathtub thoroughly, to scrub, and wash and iron. I think they find it easier to work when everything is run on an orderly basis. Every Sunday Cook and I plan the menus for the week and make out the marketing

Maureen O'Hara and Rex Harrison are the stars of the 20th Century Fox production " The Foxes of Harrow."

Steven and Odalie Fox (Rex Harrison and Maureen O'Hara) watch anxiously at the sick bed of their crippled son Etienne, played by Perry William Ward, in " The Foxes of Harrow."

list. Between pictures I find marketing quite relaxing. There are excellent markets here and I like to see anything new that comes in and to keep myself up-to-date and to know the prices. Everyone has to consider price these days, with so much demand on every salary, whether it is large or small.

We all have our favourite duties around the house—I confess I am very fussy about the linen closet. I have a list on the closet door and everything is counted when it comes from the laundry and put in its own particular place. My house is really my hobby—it takes the place of bridge and golfing . . . the one thing I really enjoy for relaxation is our swimming pool. It is essentially a family affair. We did not plan it as a background for large parties, we planned it so we could enjoy it quietly—teach Bronwyn to swim and I am persevering in trying to perfect the Australian crawl, but I am not too good. In the summer Bronwyn has her little friends in to share the fun with her.

Gardening is Will's hobby, and I admire the result of his planting and pruning. He is a born gardener—can even persuade camellias to do his will. I think I was a born scrubber- and washer-upper, even to the pots and pans. Will likes to cook and is quite a chef, but he always bows out when it comes to the washing up. He can make left-overs into party dishes and that is quite an accomplishment. With the prices of meat soaring, fish is on the menu twice a week. Will concocted a dish I think is particularly good. He uses either left-over cooked fish or slices of fresh fillets of any kind of fish. The casserole is lightly greased and he places in it a layer of fish, then a layer of thinly sliced cucumber, and repeats this to the top of the dish. He seasons it with mixed crushed herbs and a little onion; a white sauce is poured over it—enough to moisten it— and if one can spare the butter, just before it is taken from the oven a few buttered crumbs scattered over the top and browned lightly gives it an added flavour.

When we visited my husband's parents in Mississippi, which is not far from New Orleans, we had some very happy times in that fascinating place. Like all port towns, it is colourful, and its food is interesting because of the strong Creole influence. We got some very intriguing recipes, but the catch in them is that we can't find the ingredients here—we have to send to New Orleans for them.

20th Century-Fox's lovely star, Maureen O'Hara.

I haven't had much time for travelling, as my contract with 20th Century-Fox keeps me very busy. In addition, as soon as I finished " Sitting Pretty " I started work for R.K.O. in " The Long Denial," with Melvyn Douglas.

After playing several costume pictures one after the other, " Sitting Pretty " was assigned to me. It is a comedy by F. Hugh Herbert, and we really had a lot of fun making it. I played a young married woman with three children. Robert Young is my husband and the hilarious comedy situations are brought about when we engaged a baby sitter who applied for the position under the name of Lynn Belvedere.

Naturally, we never suspected it was a man, and you can well imagine the situations that came about with Clifton Webb playing the part. It turned out the baby sitter was a novelist looking for local colour. It is a picture that will have appeal all over because baby sitters have become important to families with children. I am sure its hilarious situations will have appeal, too, wherever the

23

picture is shown, especially with such a fine comedian as Clifton Webb in the baby sitter-author role.

Next comes a picture with Melvyn Douglas for R.K.O., called " The Long Denial." Its plot involves a promising young singer who loses her voice on the threshold of fame. She finds a protege whom she nurtures into the fame she herself would have had. Subsequently, to protect the girl's reputation and to save her own love affair, she risks a murder charge when her protege is shot.

Singing, by the way, is my hobby. It involves my greatest ambition—apart from being Mrs. William Price. I have been studying for years, very seriously, with the hope of singing in grand opera. My voice is a dramatic soprano. My mother was a noted opera singer of her day and had a fine contralto voice. She appeared throughout Europe in opera until her fourth baby was born ; then she had to give it up to give us her attention and to see we all had an education. We were all brought up for the theatre, and I was very proud when I earned the right to be accepted at the Abbey Theatre School and later became a member of the Theatre itself. During my early childhood I was always around the opera company with my mother and was so steeped in it I hoped that my voice would some day be good enough for me to follow my mother in her operatic career.

My husband is very sympathetic and understands what it will mean to me if I ever prove myself capable of singing Faust or Lucia Di Lammermoor—that really would be the biggest day of my career. I have three years yet to fulfil my contract with 20th Century-Fox—perhaps by that time I will be ready for the big adventure.

I have been before the public for so long, some people imagine I am much older than I am. I was a schoolgirl when I played my first part with Charles Laughton in " Jamaica Inn," and when I first came to America for " The Hunchback of Notre Dame."

So far I have never played the type of role I have really wanted to play because studios have to consider stories that they are sure have proven box office appeal, but some of the parts in plays done by the Abbey Theatre call for the type of acting I am reasonably sure I could do best.

When I first came to America I used to get much good advice and support from Olivia de Havilland, whom I admire tremendously as an actress and certainly appreciate as a friend.

I have not had too much time for the social side of life. When I first arrived in Hollywood it was all so new I had to become used to it, and I was kept very busy at the studio— and after I married I really settled down to a hundred per cent domestic life. Keeping house shared my energies with film-making and every day has been filled with my dual duties.

In spite of my gratitude for having had a career which has given me a certain amount of satisfaction and a very substantial living, I still say that if I had to make a choice between Maureen O'Hara, movie star, and Mrs. Will Price, wife and mother, I would choose to become just Mrs. Price.

Fans will remember one of Maureen O'Hara's earliest roles, that of Angharad in " How Green was My Valley."

HOLD THAT LINE!

says EDITH HEAD

Gail Russell wears a dress designed by Edith Head in her latest film " Night has a Thousand Eyes," a Paramount production. Note the New Look touches with nipped-in waistline and full, longer skirt. The material is navy blue taffeta with white silk faille collar and cuffs.

EDITH HEAD, famous Paramount designer, tells you to study line, and then you will make the best of your appearance.

EVERY woman who wants to make the best of herself should take time to study her figure with a calculating and critical eye. Few figures are perfect. Some have a short waistline that cannot be changed—it's there for life ; others have a long torso and short legs ; others have shoulders that slope too much ; others are afflicted with that bugaboo of middle age, the dowager's hump. The best can be made of any defect, but it takes a truthful summing up of one's assets and defects.

I have always believed line is the most important consideration in choosing any garment. Of next importance comes material, and, last of all, trimmings.

A designer creates, with resultant publicity, a new silhouette. If it is a well-known designer, fashionwise women begin to shop for clothes that conform to the newly launched style. Fine, if the style is meant for you, but foolish if you are just not built for the particular line decreed " the very latest."

Individualism has been my cry for a long time. Every year sees me more convinced that fashion should be slave to the woman rather than the other way round.

Let's look at styles to be well considered. For instance, the padded hip. Practically no woman needs hip padding—unless she is deformed—then padding is permissible to even things up. A bustle is advantageous to a woman who has a sway back, but bustle bows on women already well padded by nature do not look well. There is a tendency to

push draperies to the front of the skirt. This is all very well in a maternity gown but too much fullness gives too much emphasis in the wrong place. Bust lines pushed too high give a pouter pigeon effect. Waistlines should never be pushed so low that a woman looks as if she's been tied in a sack! Short-legged women should never wear skirts with drapery that goes across—horizontal pleats or tucks. Long draperies falling loosely may help lengthen the line. The sleeve should be long and slim and puffs at the wrists should be avoided. Every woman should have a long mirror and she should use it to determine the right line for her particular figure.

It is very hard to convey in words what one is driving at

Margaret Field, young Paramount player, models an ideal dinner-dance dress made of lovely lace and worn over flesh pink taffeta. The design of the lace forms a slight scallop edging to the skirt.

☆

Edith Head's basic gown lends itself to several different treatments. Margaret Field demonstrates three ways of adapting it.

☆

Bottom right is a further idea for the same gown, showing what a lot of difference you can make to your appearance by studying those small details.

in prescribing suitable fashions. That is why I believe television is a boon to designers and much more so to the woman striving to benefit by the advice of those who have learned their business well and would like to pass on their findings. When a woman watches a designer in television she can see just what that designer is doing as she talks. She does not have to imagine anything, it is demonstrated before her eyes. She sees models wearing clothes properly—the good and bad points of clothes are easily pointed out. There is no guesswork. With people getting television wise, and more sets being installed in private homes, there will be little excuse for bad dressing.

Some women are so clothes-wise they instinctively know what is right for them and what to avoid, but there are always those who just do not know how to make the best choice. Movie fans see their favourite actress wearing clothes they would like to wear. They will buy something because they saw Barbara Stanwyck wearing a similar gown. Too often they forget that perhaps it is because Miss Stanwyck's figure is just right for that particular style, and unless they have the same lines they could never achieve the same effect. I have known of petite women who insist on copying clothes worn by the rather statuesque type and

tall girls who want to look like Veronica Lake . . . that is human nature.

Another thought I would like to express is the importance of doing away with anything that is not functional. The abnormally large bag, unless you use it for carrying things—perhaps your books, or in the case of a film actress, a script, is not good. A small bag, well proportioned in regard to one's size, is much better taste.

Gloves should be worn, not carried. I have noticed some women are just perpetual glove carriers. The fingers show they have never been worn, and there is a dingy mark where they are held. Gloves should be fresh—that is why I wear black or white fabric gloves; they are easily washed. The present sleeve fashions call for short gloves, but for evening wear long gloves are very attractive. They give a good line to most arms and sometimes they do help hide neglected elbows.

In accessories, care should be taken to keep them keyed down—a good contrast is permissible—in fact, is preferable to all one tone. But it is not necessary to repeat the same colour in the hat, belt, shoes, gloves, etc., although every shade worn should harmonize.

WRONG RIGHT

Designer Edith Head shows you the wrong and right way to dress if you are the short type.

☆

Edith Head calls this the heavy type, and shows you the importance of long, sweeping lines to miss that "bulky" appearance.

☆

WRONG   RIGHT

You should wear full skirts and avoid tapering designs like the left-hand sketch if you are the tall and thin type.

Blending tones is of utmost importance and has a great deal to do with attaining the most becoming line. Colour can break a line badly so even the cut seems affected.

Here are a few of my very personal ideas I use in dressing myself : I like two sets of pockets on everything—even on my nightgowns. Since Barbara Stanwyck gave me a heavy gold bracelet with antique coins attached, I have made a collection of jewellery featuring gold coins. I never wear a hat except on trips to New York.

There are several stars who drop in to chat with me, asking advice on how to refurbish a gown or reshape a coat. Most people have to plan to make clothes do. It is no illusion that the high cost of living is affecting even well-filled pocketbooks.

WRONG   RIGHT

Rod Cameron and Jeff York in a furious fight, in the film "Panhandle."

What makes

THOUGH this is the atomic age, and television is here, movie fans still enjoy Westerns with double-holstered cowboys and wild chases, just as they did twenty years ago. You don't have to be a film mogul to discover that, because box office receipts tell the tale. The fact that studios are going in for high-budgeted outdoor dramas, and more Westerns than ever are in production, should be the convincer.

Some folks consider themselves too grown up for a Western, but I've never felt that way. Maybe I've never really outgrown my Saturday matinee days, when I used to root for Tom Mix and William S. Hart. The chases, gun duels and the scenic beauty of the spacious outdoors still excite me, and it's even much more fun when you actually become part of it.

I've never been sorry about donning high boots and a ten-gallon hat for the screen. I know fellow actors who wouldn't have anything to do with a Western if they could help it. But, believe me, they don't know what they are missing. It's a welcome relief to leave hot sound stages for the outdoors, and get paid for riding. When you make a Western you have a chance to catch up with the sun and fresh air which are practically strangers when you work behind closed doors on an indoor set.

But now I'm getting away from what I had on my mind to write about Westerns. I don't have to tell you that there's nothing new under the sun, and that plots for outdoor films were used up years ago. But isn't that true with most cinematic plots? There's usually the hero out to reach some goal, the heroine who

Three outlaws hit the dust as Rod Cameron plugs away with his six-shooters in a desperate gun battle filmed in a heavy downpour in Allied Artists' "Panhandle."

good Western

BY **ROD CAMERON**

falls for the guy, and, generally, certain characters who stand in the way of law, justice or romance. We have the same situations in Westerns, except that we actors wear cowboy outfits and rely for our scenery upon Mother Nature instead of swanky apartments and cocktail lounges.

However, in spite of an apparent similarity of all Westerns, there are those that stand out above the others when it comes to entertainment values. Take a film like John Ford's " Stagecoach." Here was a Western which was hailed in critical quarters as the best of its type ever to emerge from Hollywood. But basically it wasn't much different from the rest of the crop.

Though much of the action occurred on a stagecoach, it had the action, chase and other elements of outdoor productions. John Wayne, a hunted man fast on the trigger, proved to be the hero. Claire Trevor was the bad but good girl who wins him in the end. This takes place after a terrific chase by Indians and outlaws, plus the climaxing gun duel at the end. Top acting by Wayne, Miss Trevor, Thomas Mitchell and others in the cast raised the film above standard. The dialogue was full of punch. The suspense was sustained, even though the outlaws weren't any different from those in other outdoor epics. The photography, direction and musical background gave " Stagecoach " a vivid pace which kept one glued to one's seat until the very end.

Breaking it all down into its basic formula, action seems to be tne keynote in a Western film. That's what the fans write me, and it's apparent at the box office. They don't go for an outdoor drama that lacks action. They like it to have plenty of gun-totin' and a good fist fight. I should know about the latter because my muscles still ache from the savage battle I had with Jeff York in Allied Artists' " Panhandle." York plays a bully, an outlaw, out to see that I come to no good— and he lets me have it. Well, we had everything in that battle from jagged beer bottles to broken chairs and I can feel the lumps on my skull every time I comb my hair. But

29

A GALLERY OF WESTERNERS.
Rod Cameron.   *Murvyn Vye.*   *Gene Autry.*

that's what audiences want to see, and so we gave it to them. To be honest with you, I don't know how I came out of that fight without a couple of broken bones, even though we did use a few movie tricks.

An exciting fight is one factor that stamps a Western above par. The gun sequences, too, must be done effectively. Haphazard gun duels can hurt a production. The hero should know how to use his six-shooters, and not scatter his fire indiscriminately. Henry Fonda was typical of excellent markmanship in " My Darling Clementine," which was an outdoor film of topnotch entertainment, in my opinion. The cast and the story were both above par.

The chase is always important in an outdoor production, and a good Western is never without one. A chase, dramatically performed and depicted, adds to the film's suspense and excitement. Whether the hero is on the trail of murderers, rustlers or bandits, he should never catch them until the final reel. Sure, you know it's just about going to happen

Robert Mitchum.   *Johnny Mack Brown.*   *Roy Rogers.*

that way, but still, that's what the majority of theatregoers prefer. For instance, producers John C. Champion and Blake Edwards had me killed in the final moments of "Panhandle," but a pre preview audience didn't like the idea. Instead, I come out alive—which was to my liking. A touch of the Hitchcock in a Western will take it out of the run-of-the-mill class, and stamp it as different.

A good Western will naturally have a pretty damsel in distress, who is rescued by the hero. Though small fry don't go for Roy Rogers or Johnny Mack Brown getting mushy, I think a little of the romance angle is necessary. Maybe I'm prejudiced after having leading ladies like Yvonne De Carlo, Cathy Downs and Anne Gwynne. Too much gunplay, chasing and fighting may become a little monotonous, and a pretty face can diminish such consequences. Of course, every man to his own opinion, but I'll take romance in my outdoor films.

Comedy, too, should be included in a good Western. Characters like Gabby Hayes, Raymond Hatton and Cannonball Taylor have proved a hit as foils for Roy Rogers, Johnny Mack Brown and Jimmy Wakely, respectively. Their somewhat silly actions and gab contrast with the film's suspense, and are welcome relief if not overdone.

Photography is important, too, in an outdoor production. If the camera

Robert Preston plays the part of Murray Sinclair, one of the " bad men " in Paramount's " Whispering Smith."

31

can catch the vivid beauty of a Western sky, the windblown fields, picturesque streams and brown painted hills, the Western production will be enhanced. California, Arizona and Colorado, as well as other Western states, provide the natural background that can't be duplicated on a studio set. The stimulation offered by the beauties of nature seems to have an effect upon the actors which is reflected in more realistic performances.

Co-stars Rod Cameron and Cathy Downs on location during the filming of Rod's new Western," Panhandle."

But we can't forget music, either, for its value to a good Western drama. While some Westerns are made with singing cowboys, it's the musical background which can quicken the pace of a chase, and make an ordinary gun duel appear more suspenseful. " Stagecoach " again excelled in this The music heard in the background was perfectly timed with the action.

Of course, direction is always of ultra importance to any film, and likewise a Western will suffer if the actors are not put through their paces properly. After all, a so-called " horse opera " should not be just a routine of cowboys poking at each other or tossing guns to all points of the compass. Direction which keeps the thespians from " hamming it up," and the action within proper scope, will aid the outdoor film. A hero can be made more convincing, an outlaw more villainous and the heroine more appealing with good direction. Even the horses must appear realistic in their presentation.

A good Western, like any other fine film production, should have its harmonious combination of action, drama, romance and comedy. A tingling chase, sharp dialogue, pleasant romance and a dash of humour can make an outdoor drama above par. At least, it does from where I watch the screen.

" A good Western will have a pretty damsel in distress," says Rod Cameron. Here she is—Allied Artists' Cathy Downs.

HUMPHREY BOGART

The "Santana" and I

N EXT to an actor, I'd rather be a sailor than anything.

A sailor has all the best of it. He's a free agent and has to answer to no one except his conscience and his pocketbook, his stomach and the incredulous look on the faces of his non-sailing friends who can't believe that anybody would be so foolish as to want to spend half his life on the silly ocean.

A sailor in lots of ways is much better off than an actor. He is safer, he is freer from the restrictions of civilization, and whereas some of my friends shake a bewildered head over my nautical life, I look down my nose at them and wonder why they don't quietly chuck everything else and sail away into oblivion—well, at least until the next payment on the boat is due.

It's quite impossible to escape the instalment collector I'm told, even in a big boat. In a little one you either pay or swim. I know a man who claims he swam to Long Beach (California) from Catalina Island in record time under just such circumstances.

The " Santana "—that's my boat—is paid for (thank goodness and Jack Warner) and, barring accidents, my wife, Lauren Bacall, and I hope to be sailing her for many years to come.

I started wanting to be a sailor when I was rising ten years of age and holidaying with my parents at Seneca Point on Canandaigua Lake in upstate New York. My father gave me a one-cylinder motorboat and I used to putt-putt around the lake all day, exploring every watery inch of it. I determined then that I'd have a " real " boat. I believe my ideas went 'way beyond the yacht class. I had something in mind like a private ocean liner.

Humphrey Bogart and wife Lauren Bacall step out from their Beverley Hills home to greet a guest.

Well, I've never got the ocean liner, but I have progressed sufficiently from that one-cylinder job to be able to boast (a sailor's privilege) about the " Santana."

If it's statistics you're interested in, brother, I've got them. The " Santana " is 55 feet long. She's a 16-ton jib-headed yawl, powered by an 85-horsepower engine. Her decks are of teak, and I frequently have, and do, challenge any man to step foot on her sleek beautiful decks in anything but sandshoes. Nobody's going to scratch those shiny planks !

A good sailing boat is like a thoroughbred horse. She has a history and frequently a series of owners—and sometimes she wins races. The " Santana " has a distinguished history. She was built in 1935 for William L. Stewart, an oil company executive. Stewart won the New York-Bermuda races with her in 1937, and later placed in the Pacific races. In 1939 she was bought by George Brent, who later sold her to Ray Milland. They're actors, too.

In September, 1944 still another actor, name of Dick Powell, bought the " Santana." Then I bought her and now she's mine—and, of course, Mrs. Bogart's.

We love her. We keep her tied up neatly at Newport Beach, a yachtsmen's harbour about 55 miles from Hollywood and from the night clubs and sound stages and glamour girls. Lauren and I can handle her alone, but we keep one man, Tom Howard, as our regular skipper ; and, of course, take on a crew for any special cruise we make. Howard was a prisoner of the Japs during the war and he found that the best way to restore himself to normality was to seek the sea.

" Come on in," says ' Bogey,' " this is fine." But Lauren prefers to sun herself on the water's edge.

My wife is a good sailor. Not only that, but she looks cute in dungarees with her hair tied back, careless-like, and no make-up on. What's more important, she's good company, and that's saying a great deal when there are only two of you on the boat and you either want to talk or don't want to talk.

One of the few problems that arise from combining seamanship with acting is a problem of embarrassment. I would like to set the record straight that I am no more than an amateur sailor and I have no intention of setting myself up in competition with veteran yachtsmen and other professional boat-owners.

I was particularly embarrassed last summer when, through widely printed and widely spoken misinformation, I was expected to win the San Pedro-to-Honolulu races with the " Santana." Well, actually I was working in Warner Bros.' " Treasure of Sierra Madre " at the time, and although I had planned to race my boat, I couldn't.

But the point is that that kind of talk puts me in an awkward position with my sailing friends. Most of them are expert seamen and are inclined to curl their lips at movie people whom they consider strictly dilettantes in the sailing business.

I'm grateful to my film colony friends who touted me as the prospective winner of those races, but it didn't make me very popular with the veteran entries. It's like an amateur actor from Keokuk coming to Hollywood and announcing that he's going to win the Academy Award.

In defence of my own sailing ability, however, I'd like to report that I'm not just a sound-stage sailor. My boat (and " The Sluggy " which preceded this one) has been a familiar member of the Hollywood flotilla in the Los Angeles and Newport harbour area for a number of years. The two years I spent in the Navy during World War I, and my several years of small

Tim Holt and Humphrey Bogart in " Treasure of Sierra Madre " resting in the desert on their prospecting trip to the Sierra Madre where they believe gold will be found.

boat sailing in Californian waters have helped to give me a workable knowledge of the sea.

I even played the role of a sailor once, in a film called " Action in the North Atlantic." And I was a steamer passenger once, too—in a film called " Across the Pacific."

As a matter of fact, Lauren and I get along very well with the strange breed of folk who own and sail boats, or who borrow and sail them. People who never thought of chatting

The sea-faring Bogarts set sail on their 55-ft. yacht " Santana." Lauren is pretty handy aboard a yacht, thanks to ' Bogey's' teaching.

over the back fence with their neighbours in Hollywood or Beverley Hills get chummy as the devil with the guy in the next ship.

Just after we tied up the " Santana " the other day, I stopped to talk with a sailing neighbour at the dock next to mine. He was puttering. That's the God-given right of any boat owner. Puttering and painting are the two things he does most and best. This man was just puttering when I stopped to talk, as is the custom among boat owners and sailors.

He was friendly enough and I was non-committal, as becomes an actor who has learned when to be non-committal. I gave a bit of advice which he obviously didn't need, but didn't resent, and then I started to walk on.

Suddenly the other chap asked a question that brought me up sharply.

" Actor ? " he queried.

" Uh-uh," I said, crestfallen that he had guessed it. I'm not ashamed of my profession, but my actor's pride was hurt to think that I had tipped my mitt, as we say.

" Hollywood ? " he asked, continuing to putter.

I told him the truth. " Yes," I said.

" Talkies ? " he demanded. And I left him and walked on. I was acutely conscious that there are people in the world who don't know that " sound is here to stay."

And they're probably all boat-lovers who have other things to think about. Tides and the wind, for instance.

The Genie of Aladdin's Lamp worked for me—says Evelyn Keyes

WE all have dreams and ambitions and like most children mine took the usual fanciful, secretive form. My hopes were so far-fetched that I could not possibly share them with anyone and be considered as anything but "a strange little girl." For it was Hollywood that came to me most in my dreams.

I used to imagine myself a great actress with people waiting for me outside theatres and cafes. I saw myself smiling graciously as I signed their autograph books. As a matter of fact, after a particularly exciting day when I found it hard to go to sleep, I used to count autographs instead of sheep.

Port Arthur, Texas, was my birthplace. My father, who was in the oil refining business there, died before my first birthday. My mother took me to Atlanta, Georgia. No one minded for very long just where I was born until the genie of the lamp went to work and I began to make some progress on the screen.

Suddenly it became very important to both Texas and Georgia where I was born. Now whenever the question comes up I evade a direct answer. I am so grateful so much has happened that the two states actually are interested in claiming me.

To trace the story of the genie and me I must go back to the days when I was a gangling schoolgirl whose free hours were devoted to playing the piano and studying tap dancing. Not until after I had mastered quite a few dance steps did I let the family know that I had been dreaming of a Hollywood career.

They took it rather well and I suspect now they knew all the time. My sister sent my photograph to a Universal talent scout who was travelling through town. Imagine the excitement in the family when I was offered a screen test and imagine my own discouragement when the test brought forth nothing but a letter saying I was not quite the type for pictures !

With Hollywood ever my goal I worked on and sought as much experience as I could. I danced in night clubs and tried my best to impress the big band leaders who played in the cafes where I worked. Someone gave me a letter to Ted Fio Rito and I was certain he would be completely swept off his feet and give me " that one big chance."

In Columbia's " The Mating of Millie," Evelyn Keyes is the sort of passenger that bus-driver Glenn Ford finds difficult to handle.

Instead, the maestro gave me some advice, " Lose that Southern accent." I took it literally and worked very hard to speak with an average American accent. That accomplished I braved the studio gates of Hollywood and at long last landed my first chance in films. Why ? Because I was born in the South and Cecil B. De Mille gave me the part of a Southern belle because I could speak with a soft, low drawl ! Then came " Gone with the Wind " and again the accent was necessary. For the next part, however, I had to lose that " soft, low drawl " and I wondered just what kind of an accent I would ultimately have.

However, I have never regretted being obliging about changing my speech, for bigger and better roles started coming my way. I was under contract to Columbia and I was in the swim. I was in pictures and yes, people asked for my autograph. But having achieved this much, I soon grew restless— ambitious for that one big part. I pinned my hopes on " Here Comes Mr. Jordan " for it was such a different story from the average—one of metaphysical import. I felt that something good would come of it and something did.

The studio gave me an excellent role in " Ladies in Retirement." Then came " The Desperadoes " and everything was going beautifully. I was married to director Charles Vidor and I could feel that I had lived through many interesting moods. Then our marriage ended.

Jimmy Hunt may be small, but he plays a large role in " The Mating of Millie," with Glenn Ford and Evelyn Keyes.

I almost believed that I could find permanent happiness in building a career but as I started to play the whimsical genie in " A Thousand and One Nights " I began to realize otherwise. Like the character I played I began to wish on my own account whenever the magic lamp came into my hands. It was childish, perhaps, even silly. But now I wonder. Was it my intense wish for a richer life that brought about the elopement to Las Vegas when I married John ? Perhaps it was and perhaps the genie had more to do with it than I realize.

John had been Mr. Huston to me until I met his father, the famous actor Walter Huston, on an airplane. With understandable

parental pride he spoke at great length about his son and said that I would like to meet him. From what I heard I readily agreed. A few days later we did meet and a few months after that we were married.

We went to New York where my husband was to direct a play. Strolling along Fifth Avenue, sightseeing around New York, visiting the Metropolitan museum, the New York library and the bookshops occupied much of my time. How much there is to see if one has the opportunity.

I had been so busy preparing for Hollywood that I never had had time for books, for fine music and for art. Now there was time and I made the most of it. Besides giving me a husband, the magic lamp had given me a little leisure—something priceless to a film player.

John next went to Mexico to direct "Treasure of Sierra Madre" and I was able to go with him. Mexico is an enchanting country of incredible contrasts—wealth and poverty only inches removed from each other. The people have a curious blend of gay fiestas and grim, unending trouble in their large, expressive eyes. There is a haunting sadness about them that flees only in the momentary happiness of a song or the delight of performing a favourite dance.

For some scenes in the film we worked at the famous spa in San Jose de Perna. John and I noticed little thirteen-year-old Pablo Albarran who had become a self-appointed roustabout on the set. He carried beer and Coca Cola to the players, ran errands and took over one of the big transport trunks for his home. And with a big smile he put himself on salary when pay day came around !

Pablo and I reached a stage of friendship which took no time at all to develop into a deep affection. By the time I had to leave Mexico to return to Hollywood and start work in " The Mating of Millie " I was heartbroken at the thought of leaving the little Mexican lad behind.

John, of course, knew how I felt and it was only a matter of two days after my return that I received a wire from him saying that he, too, was on his way back to Hollywood and someone was coming with him. I knew that the " someone " could be only Pablo. My first question when I met them both at the airport was how such a miracle had been arranged.

" I enjoyed meeting Ron Randell, the young actor from Australia," says Evelyn Keyes. Ron plays the part of the head of a foundling home in " The Mating of Millie."

John had done it quite legally—by adoption. Michoacan is the one state in Mexico which does not require a long legal process for adoption. The job was done in two days.

Pablo's serape and white cotton suit and big straw sombrero have now been replaced by sweater and slacks. Shoes have been added although I must say at first they were not altogether successful. Pablo didn't know that the soles were supposed to bend and he

walked around stiff-legged for a couple of days to keep them from losing their nice new shape.

Pablo, of course, has a new name. He is Pablo Albarran Huston. He doesn't speak perfect English yet but he has a rich stock of American slang expressions, and as soon as he is sufficiently advanced in his new language, Pablo will go to school.

Pablo seems happy on our ranch in the San Fernando valley and like other boys he could never be accused of being unduly concerned with studies. He much prefers the swimming pool and going with me to the studio. And he adores watching fire engines race up and down the boulevards.

He can go to college if he chooses and if he finds himself inclined there would be no objections to his becoming an actor. Right now he shows a talent for painting—a state of affairs which pleases my husband no end.

When Evelyn Keyes and her director husband, John Huston went on location to Mexico, they met 13-year-old Pablo Albarran, an orphan. They were so taken with him that they decided to adopt him legally, and here he is in a new outfit of clothes Evelyn has just bought him.

It is probably very clear by now that my life has become a full, rich and happy one. At the studio, it seems that I am going to play the type of role which the late Carole Lombard did so beautifully and in which we all like to see Jean Arthur—the glib, wise and witty girl who gets into trouble and is rescued just in the nick of time by the handsome leading man. Such a role is the one I am playing in " The Mating of Millie." Glenn Ford is wonderful to work with and I enjoyed meeting Ron Randell, the young actor from Australia.

As " Millie " I play the role of a department store executive who wants to adopt an orphaned boy but can't because she isn't married. Glenn Ford is the bus driver I try to lure into a marriage " in name only." He refuses, but agrees to aid me nevertheless, by helping me find another man. This search accomplishes Millie's transition from a severe, matter-of-fact young woman into a butterfly who finds that she has missed a great deal in by-passing femininity.

For my part as a personnel manager of a big store I spent several weeks in the offices of a downtown Los Angeles store learning how to talk like an executive and how to dress for the part.

Glenn Ford actually drove a bus for a transit company in Santa Monica before he became an actor and when he took the wheel of one of the big buses we used in the picture he went at the job as though he had never missed a day from his old occupation.

All of the players in the picture did research for their roles—all except Jimmy Hunt, the seven-year-old actor who plays the orphan boy in the picture. Jimmy, tow-headed, blue-eyed and adorable, needed to know nothing. Just by being himself I am quite sure he has stolen the picture from his elders. He never muffs a line or misses a cue and of course he never hesitates to correct others' mistakes.

THE STORY OF A GREAT STUDIO

by David Hanna
Film Critic, The Hollywood Daily Reporter

Universal Studio as it looked in 1915. Insets L.-R.: Tom Mix, Lon Chaney and Mary Pickford, who brought fame and fortune to Universal in its early days.

THE oldest motion picture company in Hollywood goes by the name of Universal-International. Its stars are many and great ; its executive roster lists men of splendid reputation and its affiliation with J. Arthur Rank gives it particular eminence in movie circles. But there was a day when its name bore no hyphen ; when it was called simply, Universal, and it was presided over by a man of short stature but with a big heart. He was Carl Laemmle, an immigrant boy from Germany, who wandered one day in 1893 into the Chicago World's Fair and saw Edison's Kinetoscope. The youngster never forgot the machine with the jumping photographs and because of that youthful impression he lived to write a vibrant, glowing, exciting chapter as the most intrepid of the motion picture pioneers.

Twelve years later, young Carl was in business for himself—operating a ten cent store in Chicago. Down the street was a makeshift theatre with an entrance on one side, an exit on the other and box-office in the middle. He noticed the stream of customers constantly going into the " store shows " and before long Carl was in show business himself. Because it became difficult to obtain products he decided to go into production himself and like the other motion picture experimenters he started out in New York.

Soon thereafter the movie migration to California was in full swing. Film producers were moving westward to the Golden State where nature provided an endless variety of scenery and constant sunshine. Laemmle's Universal joined the procession and in 1912, it erected a studio in the village of Hollywood.

Film business was good and getting better. Theatres mushroomed throughout the land. Western pictures, movies with cowboys, Indians and bandits, caught the public fancy. There was a growing demand for serial thrillers. Custard pie comedies added a new and merry splash to the era. Within a couple of years, Universal needed more room and Laemmle who now was known as " Uncle Carl " moved to the valley where he built the first large motion picture studio. The area was named Universal City and it included a residential section, a post office, its own fire department and civic administration.

On this site, Universal-International flourishes to-day—a series of buildings and sound stages rambling leisurely across the countryside. The main street is paved now and bright, little shops serve the thousands of workers. The residential area is nearby—all very prim and proper—a far cry from those early days when the Indians who appeared in Universals' movies actually lived in tepees and cowboys erected their own bunkhouses.

The founder of Universal, Carl Laemmle.

The 300 foot long, roofless platforms could hardly be called film stages when judged by modern standards. But they were picturesque. Overhead, to diffuse the dazzling sunlight, were huge muslin screens strung on wires and on them directors shouted, pistols popped and lovers made love —at one and the same time. Amplifying the tumult were the spectators—the " rubbernecks " who paid " two bits " a head to come in and watch them make the movies. The sightseers cheered and applauded from bleacher seats built atop the dressing rooms. Those were bright, uninhibited days at Universal City as the movie industry grew out of its swaddling clothes into infancy and finally, manhood.

As the films grew in world-wide stature and more and more people came to regard the " flicks " their best and cheapest form of entertainment, so did Universal grow. The big names began to join Uncle Carl. Anna Pavlova did " The Dumb Girl of Fortici " and Mae Murray came to prominence in " Princess Virtue." Others of his stars were Dorothy Phillips, Harry Carey, Herbert Rawlinson, Ella Hall, Grace Cunard, Fritzi Brunette, the child star Zoe Rey, Jack Holt and Priscilla Dean, the great lady of the serials.

Pictures were turned out at an enormous rate. In one year alone some 250 features passed before Universal's cameras. And the titles were as bold as Uncle Carl could make them. Without blushing, he sent forth " Scandal Mongers," " Virgin of Stamboul," " The Heart of Humanity " and the famous celluloid shocker of World War I, " The Kaiser, Beast of Berlin." Occasionally there were " classics " such as " Under Two Flags " and " Twenty Thousand Leagues Under the Sea " but in the main, the movie diet consisted of cops and robbers and unsullied maidenhood. The public didn't seem to care so long as the movies were there to entertain them.

The twenties brought forward another development in the rise of Universal. Laemmle had made experiments in indoor shooting and came to the realization that economies could be effected and wider latitude of background achieved if films could get inside out of the sun. Sound stages with roofs was the next step and among the most impressive built at this time was the famous " Phantom " set.

It was a reproduction of the Paris Opera House which forms the background of the famed horror story, " The Phantom of the Opera "—a picture which brought international fame to character actor, Lon Chaney.

Pictures that talked were the next steps in the evolution of films and Uncle Carl was caught with the biggest silent spectacle of his career. Undaunted by the new invention he simply added sound effects and " Showboat " went into release with Joseph Schildkraut, billed as " the world's most beautiful man," playing Gaylord Ravenal, the charming gambler of the Mississippi.

Laemmle was quick to recognize the importance of sound and it was only a matter of months before Paul Whiteman, the beloved American jazz man, was doing a picture titled, appropriately, " The King of Jazz." And it was at this time that Uncle Carl made the one mighty film of his career, " All Quiet on the Western Front "—an anti-war film with an unknown cast. It was expensive ; it was risky. But the producer who came from the same Germany that had declared war on his adopted land had something more on his mind than Indians and cowboys and sophisticated Parisian boudoir comedies.

He saw " All Quiet on the Western Front " through to completion and whoever saw it then remembers it today—remembers it as one of the finest motion pictures of all time. And in the list of great movie scenes, no old-timer ever forgets that in which Lew Ayres reached a hand out of a trench in no man's land to pluck a flower, only to draw back his fingers dripping with blood put there by a machine gun volley.

Yes, Uncle Carl had his way and " All Quiet " more than fulfilled his fondest dreams. It was a hit and he was ready to go on to new pictures and new stars—Norman Kerry, Clara Bow, Dolores Del Rio, Wallace Beery, Irene Dunne, John Boles, Laura La Plante and Paul Robeson.

But it was inevitable that the day would come when Uncle Carl had outlived his usefulness—when the city he had built would become too big—even for him. For some years, Universal had been losing money and of course it had to be someone's fault. Since Uncle Carl ran things, he was the gentleman responsible. On Laemmle's resignation, Nate Blumberg and Cliff Work, two men from the theatre field, assumed control. Within recent years they have been joined in the management of the company by three respected production men, Leo Spitz, Cheever Cowdin, and William Goetz. Implemented by its distribution arrangement with J. Arthur Rank, Universal-International is again at the top.

The main entrance of Universal Studios as it is to-day.

All my friends
by SHIRLEY TEMPLE AGAR

SINCE you have asked me to write this story about " neighbours " the first thing I have to tell you (because I'm still so excited about it) is that the newest " neighbour " in the Agar household is Jack's and my tiny daughter, born Friday, January 30th, 1948.

I like to think of almost everybody being a " neighbour," and a neighbour for a long time. People who are well past middle-age still come up to me on the street and say, " So you're Shirley Temple. I used to see you in pictures when *I* was a little girl." That may sound a little strange since I'm only now going on twenty years of age, but I don't mind at all and I like to think that they *have* known me for a long time.

When I married Jack Agar on September 19th, 1945 I gained a lot of new " neighbours." Jack has a large family—some of whom I haven't been able to meet yet because they live in the East and they too, will, I hope, all be loving " neighbours."

Just being married gives you lots of new " neighbours." For instance, the girls I met at the cooking school I attended after my marriage. Up until that time I had no idea, I must admit, even how to boil an egg.

Shirley Temple, Victor McLaglen and John Agar (Shirley's husband) star in Argosy's picture " Fort Apache."

are Neighbours to me

So by now I hope and guess you've gathered that I don't just count as " neighbours " the people who live on our street. All my friends abroad—whom I enjoy so much receiving letters from—I consider my " neighbours." The definition of " neighbour " I'd like to think is that every person in the whole world is a neighbour to every other one.

As far as the common meaning of " neighbour " is concerned, I guess Zazu is our closest one . . . in more ways than one. It was through her that I first met my husband, Jack. But I can't go on talking about " neighbours " for ever and, besides, I'd like to tell you all a little bit about what Jack and I have been doing the past year or so.

One of the most important things is that Jack has just finished his first picture, " Fort Apache," and I was chosen to play the girl in the picture after Jack had been cast as the romantic lead. Everyone says he's wonderful in it—naturally, I think so—and I hope you will like him.

And then we have our own beautiful home now in West Los Angeles. It's English cottage style, incidentally, and I had a wonderful time working with the interior decorator fixing it up. Downstairs in the playroom—now protected by light wooden panels—I have my wonderful doll collection—from " neighbours " all over the world. We use that room, too, for our little dances and bridge parties.

Jack and I only began playing bridge a few months ago and we really love it. I've made great strides in it, too, because when we first started Jack refused to have me as his partner—was afraid I'd trump his ace or something. But in the last few weeks—I think it dates from the time I bid and made a grand slam—he looks more kindly upon me as his partner.

Of course in the recent past I wasn't able to do much of anything but

In " Fort Apache," Shirley and her husband, John Agar, are teamed together for the first time.

just wait for the baby. So I spent most of my time knitting and reading. We belong to the Book-Of-The-Month Club and that makes reading a very easy relaxation in the Agar household. But even during the past few months I haven't been able to read a book without thinking about how it would be on the screen. This is only the second time in my life when I haven't worked for about a year. When I went to Westlake School for Girls I didn't make a picture, either, for about a year.

And although I enjoy the change of being home for a while and am a mother now, I don't want to give up acting. Oh, I won't go back to work probably for several months at least until my baby and I get to know each other really well but then I'd like to return to pictures.

I think it's a wonderful life, to be a movie actress. And while we're on this subject many people have asked me, would Jack and I approve of a life in pictures for our child. We've talked this over and if she wants to become an actress as she grows older, or shows a great aptitude for it as a youngster, we certainly won't talk her out of it. I feel I had a very rich, full life being a movie child—but still a life in the basic things that was no different from any other child's.

Another thing we want to do—and this is in the pretty far off future—is some travelling. For instance, I've never been abroad, neither has Jack, and we both want to do that. We can see some of our European " neighbours "—just to keep on the subject—then. But that won't come until after we've done some visiting through our own country. Jack's never seen much of California—Lake Arrowhead, Yosemite Valley, Lake Tahoe and I haven't done much travelling through the East. Particularly I want to visit Texas, Illinois and New Jersey where portions of Jack's large family live.

I'd also like to take up my golf and French conversation lessons again. The former I began, just to end being a golf widow, but then got really to enjoy it. Jack loves to play—shoots in the low seventies—and was always missing from home golf club way. When, for one Christmas, he gave me a beautiful matching set of clubs, I got the hint and began golf lessons.

As far as the French lessons go, those were started when I was very young, but I never stuck at it long enough really to be able to carry on an intelligent—or even

understandable conversation for any length of time. I had just started again with vim and vigour when I began making " Fort Apache," and, of course, had to give them up. But soon now I hope I'll be able really to " jabber " away—in French.

But, most of all, what I want to do now is make life happy for my husband and little baby girl, Linda Susan Agar.

Shirley and John Agar, her husband in real life, went, with Henry Fonda and other stars, to an Indian Reservation in Arizona and New Mexico for the shooting of " Fort Apache."

CHARLIE McCARTHY AND EDGAR BERGEN

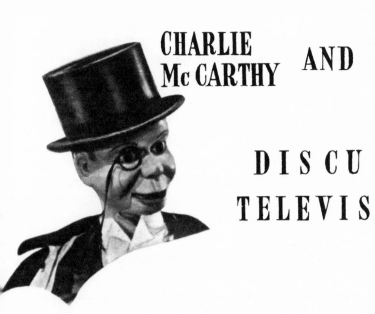

DISCUSS TELEVISION

BERGEN : Well, Charlie, just think, in another year or two, with the new television sets, people will be able to see us as well as hear us, in their homes.

CHARLIE : That ought to break up a lot of homes.

BERGEN : No, seriously Charlie, times are changing. We've got to think about the future. What do you think will happen to all our established screen and radio stars ?

CHARLIE : Bergen, I'm glad you asked that. It so happens—just by the merest chance, mind you—that I've worked out an entire flock of predictions along these lines.

BERGEN : Where do I figure in these predictions ?

CHARLIE : With your figure, Mr. Bergen, I thought it would be kinder to leave you out entirely. Mind you, I don't say television is going to kick over the radio and screen rackets completely, but I think things will happen along the following lines :

1. I predict that Don Ameche will either have to change his brand of toothpaste or a lot of television listeners are going to have to buy smoked glasses.

2. I predict that Orson Welles will scare more people with his neckties than his " Invasion from Mars " broadcast did several years ago.

3. Now that Lassie has his own radio show, I predict the first big animal television star will be a cat. You can leave him on all night and frighten the mice.

4. I predict that daytime dramatic serials won't get as much sympathy from the housewives as they used to. When you see some of the people who appear in them, you'll realize they deserve to suffer much more than they do.

5. I predict a great upswing in toupee sales for actors going into television. Bergen has already ordered three special dome doilies—one windswept one for outdoor roles, one oiled and polished for night club scenes, and one emotionally disturbed toupee, in case he should get an acting part opposite Bette Davis.

6. I predict television sets won't offer very good reception when Gregory Peck makes an appearance, because too many of the listening ladies will be generating electrical interference of their own.

7. For people who love to eat in movie theatres, I predict television will meet this challenge with a combination receiving set, cook stove, and refrigerator all built into one unit.

8. I predict other television sets will be equipped with wind-shield wipers for folks who like to hiss such villians as Peter Lorre and Boris Karloff.

9. I predict actors with character in their faces should make a lot of money in television. Someone with bags under their eyes and the complexion of Fred Allen, say, could be turned sideways, and used as a backdrop for a Hawaiian sunset.

10. I predict television will solve a lot of family problems. When bobby-soxers swoon at the sight of Sinatra or Como now, their parents can simply pick them up, carry them upstairs, and get them to bed at a respectable hour for a change.

11. I predict television will create a lot of new stars—for a lot of new reasons. For instance, a television leading man may become a favourite with housewives overnight, simply because his complexion matches the curtains in the front room.

12. I predict television will help the problem of insects in many homes. Imagine how moths will dash their little selves to pieces against the television screen trying to get at one of Crosby's sports coats.

13. Some screen stars are either going to have to tone down their romantic technique, or else a lot of homes will have to change over to higher voltages. A Gable love scene with Lana Turner will probably fuse the electrical wiring in a lot of houses.

14. For people who like the illusion of sitting in a theatre while seeing a dramatic show, television will have to answer to that, too. I predict that some sets will have special equipment that blows a draught on your feet, crackles sweet papers, and occasionally tosses an empty peanut shell at you.

15. I predict that soon after television is established, something new will be invented, " Smellevision," in which you will not only be able to see and hear, but also smell your favourite show. (Or have you been getting the same effect lately, anyway ?)

In smellevision, you will not only be able to hear news broadcasts with an eye-witness describing " flying saucers," but you will be able to smell his breath at the same time.

*   *   *

Yes sir, it's going to be a great old world to-morrow, with all these new gadgets coming in. Anyone know where I can buy a one-way ticket on a rocket ship to Mars ?

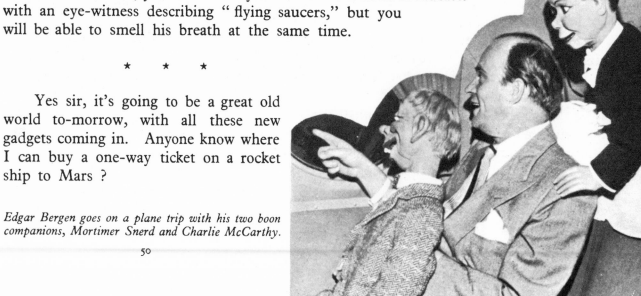

Edgar Bergen goes on a plane trip with his two boon companions, Mortimer Snerd and Charlie McCarthy.

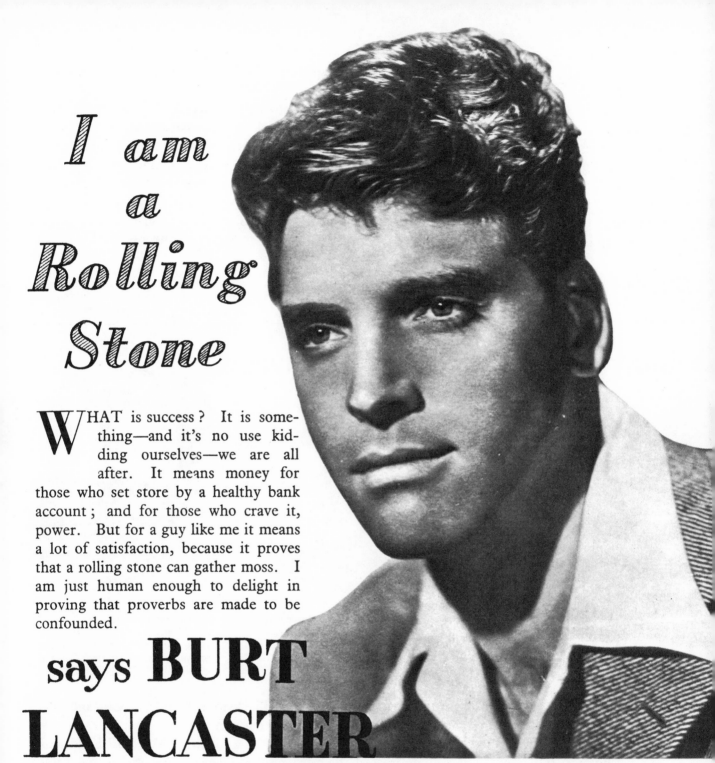

I am a Rolling Stone

WHAT is success? It is something—and it's no use kidding ourselves—we are all after. It means money for those who set store by a healthy bank account; and for those who crave it, power. But for a guy like me it means a lot of satisfaction, because it proves that a rolling stone can gather moss. I am just human enough to delight in proving that proverbs are made to be confounded.

says BURT LANCASTER

But two men had a lot to do with stopping the stone, meaning me, from rolling too long and too far: one is Hal Wallis, Hollywood producer of " Sorry, Wrong Number," and many other films; and the other is the late Mark Hellinger, beloved story writer, producer of " The Naked City," and a man cut off much too soon from his life so rich in its understanding of men and in helping those on the uphill climb to reach the heights he had already reached. All who knew him mourn Mark Hellinger. I had good reason to appreciate him for it was he who came to Hal Wallis and asked that I might play in

" The Killers " and it was in this film I won my spurs as a motion picture actor, and another contract.

Since I arrived in Hollywood I have to a certain degree overcome the restlessness that made my early life one of " chop and change." I was foolish enough—or was it foolishness ?—to give up my school books and a college education for a fling at circus life. I was at college when the urge to join a circus hit me so hard I signed on with Kay Brothers, a small circus travelling around New York State. I was born on Manhattan Island, so I was not too far from home ; but after I had a taste of small circus life I wanted to move on to the " big top," so I joined Ringling Bros. for a time—then followed vaudeville engagements. I appeared in night clubs and in some of the big hotels in an

Paramount's rugged new screen favourite, Burt Lancaster, keeps fit by playing golf.

" I wonder where that one went to ! " says Burt on No. 1 tee.

Seated on a bridge in Arizona are Wendell Corey (left) and Burt Lancaster, gazing at the passing clouds during a lull in the shooting of " Desert Fury."

acrobatic act. After doing flip-flops at the Drake and Blackstone Hotels in Chicago and playing other Mid-Western hotels, I decided I had had enough.

I wanted to learn how truck drivers fare, so I asked for a job with Marshall Field and Co., but my rather well-cut suit impressed the personnel manager : he offered me a job in the sales department. To my amusement, I was put to work as a floorwalker—the irony of ending up in this job when all I wanted was a truck driving billet. Well, I seemed to be more adapted to floorwalking than I thought—later I became top salesman. I became bored with the job and I am ashamed to say I resorted to such schoolboy antics as suddenly walking on my hands in the aisle— I thought, this will do it, they will fire me ! But no, they glossed over the untoward happening. But I was so fed up I resigned. Then I jumped around from job to job until I joined the army. That I had to, and did, take seriously.

The war over, with my discharge in my pocket, I thought I would start looking for something in radio. In the elevator on my way up to see an agent, some man in the elevator—later I learned he was an agent—thought I was just the type for the role of Sergeant Mooney in " A Sound of Hunting." He followed me into the office I was headed for and then and there insisted I should have an audition. I got the part and so started my acting career. After having several pictures marked up to my score, I know that old restlessness of mine was no adolescent trait. It surges within me constantly, but is tempered by a realization of responsibility.

Marriage has steadied me down. My wife has good, sound judgment and has the unbelievable wisdom of waiting until she is asked for an opinion. She has my unstinted

Burt is a handy man around the house, and enjoys working and tinkering with tools.

When you have been a circus acrobat like Burt Lancaster, the habit of keeping fit stays, and there is no better way than with a baseball and a bat.

Burt's new film, his own production, will be " Kiss the Blood off my Hands." He came to Hollywood via the Broadway stage, as did Vic Mature, another he-man.

admiration for her gift of restraint. I met my wife in an overseas U.S.O. show—but after we married she said she had had her professional fling and was quite happy to sit on the sidelines while I had mine.

She is very interested, too, in all my ambitions—so much so that I have named my company, Norma Productions, after her. The first production will be Gerald Butler's story, " Kiss the Blood Off My Hands." Norman Foster will direct and the cast chosen is practically all British.

My new seven-year contract with Hal Wallis gives me the privilege of making outside pictures as well as having a fling at production, so it is really a grand set-up for a fellow of my restless spirit.

In " Sorry, Wrong Number," which I am making at the time of this writing,

I have actually graduated to wearing a suit, collar and tie—heretofore I have been such a tough guy on the screen I have worn dungarees, sweat shirts or convicts' stripes. In this film, I at least have the veneer, but it must be confessed it is only just that, for again I turn out to be a killer. I have yet to behave like a gentleman for my audiences.

After my present contract ends, about seven years from now, what next? I have done more than a little introspection to determine just what causes this seething unrest. Lots of fellows have it, but not many to the degree it bothers me. Searching back into my ancestry (something I have never bothered too much about), the more genealogically inclined members of the Lancaster family tell me we go back to the House of Lancaster. Be that as it may, perhaps my questions as to my own nature are answered in their finding that the explorer Stanley was an ancestor. That might account for the urge I have for new fields and places. I rather liked it, too, when they included Field Marshal Roberts of Boer War fame somewhere along the family tree. " Fighting Bob "—what a man he was—I can remember hearing tales told of him in his campaigning days. I actually looked up the poem Rudyard Kipling wrote about him. I kept my pride to myself in hearing I was of the same strain as the grand old soldier, as here in America there is not quite the same pride of family that exists in England, it is not emphasized, but there is in all of us a pride of race, I don't mind admitting it.

Unfortunately life now rushes along at such a clip there is little time even for the amenities; and the only pride that shows itself is in the achievement of the moment or the accumulation of wealth. In my case I get a glow if I feel I have passed muster in playing a character, and a very private glow comes when I can dive into the ocean without too much terror of the water. I was trapped once as a kid under a pier. It was pitch black, and when I realized the little space there was in which to keep my head above water, I was so panicky I had a hard time getting out and swallowed plenty of that rather filthy water. Since then I have had an inordinate fear of water which I tried to lick by qualifying as a lifeguard, but the deeprooted fear comes popping up when least expected, but I summon pride enough to dive in.

Lizabeth Scott and Burt Lancaster made a splendid combination in their two films " Desert Fury " and " I Walk Alone."

Warner Bros'. star Janis Paige introduces the new "Hair-O'-Plenty" coiffure created by Perc Westmore, head of the studio's hairdress and make-up department.

The Westmore Saga

by Perc Westmore

THE paths to Hollywood are many and devious, but I seriously doubt that any can equal the Westmore Saga for circuitous approach, an approach directly traceable to the wanderlust and driving ambition of my father, George Westmore.

Father was born on the Isle of Wight, and his first job was that of lather boy (assistant or helper to a barber). At that time the assistant to a barber not only was the mixer of lather in a mug but a bootblack; and a business man would call for his barber instead of patronizing the shop. At the customer's office the barber would hone and strop the razors while the lather boy would shine the patron's shoes and mix the lather. The barber then would perform the duties of shaving and haircutting.

After Dad qualified as a barber, he became an apprentice hair-dresser and passed through the London Academy of Hairdressing, which was the ultimate schooling of all fine, male European hairdressers.

In 1908 the Westmore family started on the first lap of a journey that eventually was to land them in Hollywood. We emigrated to Montreal, Canada, the family then consisting of Dad and Mother, Mont, Wally, my twin brother Ern, and myself. From Montreal we moved on to Toronto, and eventually to Quebec, dividing our period of residence among these three cities until 1913.

Then came the momentous decision to seek our fortune in the United States. Our entrance was from Winnipeg to St. Louis; from St. Louis we moved to Cleveland, Ohio.

Ours was the typical English household. At table, Mother sat facing Father at the head. Each of us children had his turn at setting the dinner table. There was one thing we never enjoyed placing within reach of my father's right hand, and that was his favourite razor strop. He was a stern disciplinarian and needed never to ask my Mother

The Westmores, Hollywood's great family of make-up experts, as they looked in 1931. Perc is second from left.

who deserved " correction " for any particular actions of the day. His glance would rove around the table and recognize a guilty look immediately. Mother would be called upon to name the charges. He would then dole out punishment to the culprit. Punishment ranged from bed without dinner, a couple of good swats with the strop, denial of our privileges or pleasures for a specified length of time, a week's dish-washing, and other irksome household chores.

One particular evening in Cleveland (I was twelve years old), my father came home and asked the question that was to light the way for us. " Which one of you children would like to become a wigmaker and hairdresser ? " We all looked at one another, and

after a few moments of silence I raised my hand. Admiration of my father's reputation as a great hairdresser prompted me. To be like him, I thought, would be a wonderful achievement.

My father said, " You'll go with me to-morrow (Saturday) morning to the beauty parlour." My thought was that I would start off with hair work. Much to my chagrin, my father's first order at the beauty parlour was that I wash out the basins, clean the rats out of the basement, and re-arrange all plaster cast heads of baldheaded clients and put them in numerical order. This procedure took place every Saturday for the entire school

Perc Westmore gives great care and attention to Bette Davis' lips. He has been head of make-up at Warner Bros. for several years.

term until summer vacation. Father then got me a job with Carl Fickard's conservative wig house as an apprentice in the workshop. Mr. Fickard's first instruction to his apprentice included an appreciation of the fact that my father understood the hair business—and he didn't want me to take any hair home in my pockets !

After working there for two months, I was called into his office and accused of stealing hair. I denied it. I said, " I remember what you told me and appreciate the fact that father likes hair, but I have never stolen any." A sense of deep injustice accompanied me as I left for lunch. Upon my return, I noticed a rat running across the floor with a piece of raw hair in its mouth, and watched it disappear under a big wig-drying oven. I moved the oven away from the wall, and there lay several pounds of hair in countless shades. I called Mr. Fickard. " You have been missing hair and accusing me of stealing." I showed him what I had found. Raw hair is stored in oatmeal and the rats had been stealing the hair for an oatmeal diet !

That evening, I told my father the story with the result that he wouldn't allow me to return to work. He decided that I should stay at home, and practise wigmaking under his instruction after school.

We lived in Cleveland for two years, moved on to San Antonio, to New Orleans (where my brother, Bud, was born), to Washington, D.C., back to Cleveland, and then to Pittsburgh.

In San Antonio, however, I became a bootblack. It was in this Texas city that my father first opened his own place of business in the United States, and Ern and I acted alternately as caretakers and bootblacks, shining ladies' shoes in the beauty parlour.

It was in Pittsburgh that my father and I worked in competitive beauty parlours ; and Dad for the first time conceived the idea of making wigs at home. I was told to quit my job, and he built a wig shop in our attic. There, I was chained by the ankle to the work bench. Dad was taking no chances of my *not* becoming a wigmaker.

I worked at my attic work bench from 8 a.m. to 9 p.m. daily ; and was allowed a picture show once a month. Naturally, I rebelled. Accordingly, I was forced to work at the bench without my shoes, the premise being that even should I get free from the chain, I couldn't go out.

We remained in Pittsburgh for six or seven months, and left over-night in a Maxwell touring car for California. My father was a man of quick decisions.

It took us three and a half months to get to California.

In Colorado, we were caught in a terrific flood. Because the water was up to the running board and the car stalled, Dad took out the tyre chains and made us boys take off our shoes and stockings and pull the car through the water.

In crossing, we burned off an axle in St. Louis. In this city, too, Mother became ill, so Dad sent her and Dorothy on ahead of us to San Diego by train. Between St. Louis and Hisperia, California, we burned out nine axles.

We drove into the City of Los Angeles on the night of July 5th and parked at Busch's Gardens, then an auto camp in Pasedena. We had exactly $4.15 between us. Luck was with us, however, for that very week Father, Ern, and I went to work for the Paris Hair Company, accumulating sufficient money in the first few working days to get a hotel room to enable the entire family to have a bath.

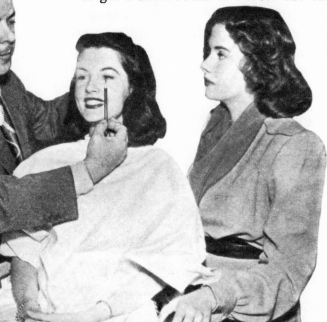

The following week we pooled wages to rent a house on the south side of Los Angeles and bring Mother and Dorothy on from San Diego.

Wally soon went to work in the L. A. Sash and Door Works as a carpenter. Ern decided he didn't like wig-making,

In the studio at Warner Bros., Helen Westcott watches closely as Barbara Bates has her make-up applied by Perc Westmore. Perc is showing here how to determine perfect proportion between the nose and the eyebrows ; when a pencil is placed perpendicularly at the outside of the nostril, the point of the pencil should indicate the beginning of the eyebrows.

59

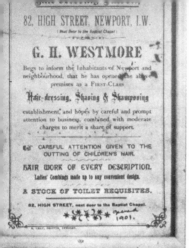
A memento of the days when George Westmore opened his first beauty shop in Newport, Isle of Wight, in 1901.

and became a Maxwell car salesman. Mont became a plumber, and I continued with my hair work.

Eventually we pooled resources again to buy lumber and a lot. My Father hired a carpenter and he, Dad, and us kids built a California bungalow in one day on West Adams Street. That house, incidentally, still stands.

Because we had a bit of land around the house, Dad decided that we should raise rabbits. During the time we lived there (a period of eight months to a year), we sold Young's Market twelve to fifteen hundred pounds of rabbits every Thursday.

Dad in the meantime had joined Maison Cesare as a hairdresser and wigmaker, and I went to work at the same place as a ventilator (putting hair into a foundation). After a few months, Dad again changed employers, going to work for Hepner's. Again, I joined him.

It was at Hepner's that the incident took place that proved to be the " open sesame " for the Westmore family to the motion picture business.

Along with my other duties, I reached the shop as early as six-thirty every morning to sweep out. One morning before my Father had arrived, there was a frantic knocking on the door. I opened it to a harassed gentleman who gasped, " Where's the wigmaker ? I've shaved off my moustache by mistake, and am due on the studio set in a half hour ! " The distraught gentleman was Adolphe Menjou, then at work in Douglas Fairbanks, Sr.'s " The Three Musketeers." There was nothing for it—I took Menjou back to the wig room and made a matching half of a moustache.

When Menjou arrived late on the set, he explained to Fairbanks what had happened Fairbanks was so impressed with the natural appearance of the moustache that he stopped work on the production, although it had been under way for two weeks, and commissioned my Father and me to make new wigs and hairpieces for the cast principals.

In visiting the set in connection with his hair-work, Dad became interested in motion picture make-up. At that time, all actors and actresses applied their own make-up. Thinking of the dangers of daily variability in application because of individual mood, the idea of studio make-up men was born in him.

Accordingly, he called all of his sons together and we began nightly experimentation in the evolvement and application of screen make-ups. Dad's first job as a make-up artist was for the Norma Talmadge Company and First National Pictures; and he set about making a studio make-up artist indispensable. From this early realization and ambition on his part the studio make-up business grew into to-day's proportions. George Westmore was truly the father of the motion picture make-up business.

Now, his boys are carrying on the profession of their Father on a scale unthought of in his day. Wally is in charge of make-up at Paramount, Bud is in the same position at Universal-International, Frank and Ern are at Eagle Lion, and for years I have headed the make-up department of Warner Bros.

The foyer of the famous Westmore salon in Hollywood, to-day.

For You — NEW FACES

MICHAEL NORTH   DORIS DAY   JAMES MITCHELL

by Michael Curtiz

NOT quite two years ago, when I decided to go into independent production with my own company, entitled Michael Curtiz Productions, I decided that I should have stronger motive than the mere act of going into picture-making for myself.

As a director for the greater portion of my life, long ago I had come to the conclusion that motion pictures had become too tied to the star system, and that it was time that those of us who love the profession should do something about it.

We had been making one picture after another with the same stars who had proven box-office appeal, and this selective problem wasn't exactly one of our own making. Unless the picture was labelled as what is known as a " sleeper " without important box-office names, people stayed away from the theatres in droves.

Too many movie-goers choose their film-fare by the names of the players rather than the possible entertainment value of the plot alone, and those of us who were going into independent production knew that sooner or later we would face this dilemma.

However, after some comparisons and considerable analysis, I reasoned that if the Broadway stage could produce successful plays with comparative unknowns in the leading roles, the arguments favoured the fact that it could also be done on the screen.

So, when I began to cast my first independent production " The Unsuspected," I decided that I would cast a new and fresh personality in the role of the young leading man. When the news was circulated in Hollywood, my hunt began. There was considerable agreement and a definite acknowledgment of the fact that the film industry needed new faces.

Not that I was being a pioneer with a startling innovation ; it was merely that for a long time I, too, had felt the need for a change, but like so many others in Hollywood, I had done nothing about it. Now I had my opportunity with my first production, and it was a challenge which I was eager to take up. Naturally there were some pre-requisites for the kind of man I wanted. Above all, I felt that a good personality was much more important than talent, although a happy combination would have been more than welcome.

In my years in the picture business, I had

Fred Clark (left), one of Michael Curtiz's new faces, plays a friendly, easy-going detective in "The Unsuspected," with Claude Rains and Audrey Totter.

discovered that so many attractive young people who came to me with high hopes were the victims of overtraining. They had gone to acting schools, where they had lost their complete sense of naturalness, and had become stagey and affected.

This was the first thing I sought to avoid, and as the candidates for the role in " The Unsuspected " came to my office, it was apparent that entirely too many youngsters were the products of these schools. I was looking for a new personality, and all I got was a procession of young men and women who were following the set patterns of Hollywood.

Then along came a young man who was handsome without being aware of it, and whose charming personality and modest bearing made an instant impression on me. Furthermore, he did not ask for the leading part, but rather asked if he would be considered for a smaller role which he had heard was open.

This was a rare phenomenon in a business where most candidates want to start at the top, so I was doubly interested. I asked the lad to read for me, and my first conviction that he might be the leading man for whom I was searching was proved. He read with a quiet and sincere dignity, and soon sold himself to me.

If you have seen " The Unsuspected," you will know that this man's name is Michael North. My faith in him was rewarded because, although he was a comparative beginner in the acting business, he held his own with veteran Claude Rains and such experienced performers as Constance Bennett and Joan Caulfield.

Next you will see him in a musical which is now in preparation, and the mention of this film brings to mind my second new face for you, a vivacious blonde named Doris Day. At first glimpse she reminds you of many a girl you've known in your own neighbourhood.

She isn't what you'd call a raving beauty, according to the standards by which we measure models, but she has a winsome, buoyant spirit, and a generous personality which wins you over from the very first moment. And she has a singing voice that carries a warm and personal message.

You'll see her in my next production, " Romance on the High Seas," and I know you'll like her. As a matter of fact, I don't know of anyone who isn't enthusiastic about her, both on and off the screen, and a half-dozen publications have applauded her by listing her as the best bet for stardom in 1948.

Fred Clark, my third new face, was the result of a search for a man to play a new kind of screen detective in " The Unsuspected." I didn't want the usual snappy, fast-talking character who is quick on the trigger and knows all the answers.

I wanted my detective to be a friendly, somewhat easy-going man, much like the type you are apt to find in any metropolitan police station. He should be a man who, at six in the evening, goes home to his family and becomes just another member of the community. I certainly didn't want him to be the epitome of the cinema criminologist.

Director Michael Curtiz doesn't believe in being tied to the star system. He is always on the watch for new faces.

My search ended almost before it began, because one night I was attending a summer theatre play at Laguna Beach, California, and there on the stage was exactly the man I wanted. He played my kind of detective, and before I left that theatre I had signed him to a contract without a screen test.

My newest face belongs to a New York stage actor named James Mitchell, who's so new that not many people have seen even his picture.

I saw him in a Broadway production entitled " Brigadoon," and, like Fred Clark, I knew he was the man for a leading role in my third production, a Technicolor epic of the California Gold Rush entitled " The 49'ers."

I hope film audiences will endorse my efforts to bring fresh personalities to the screen.

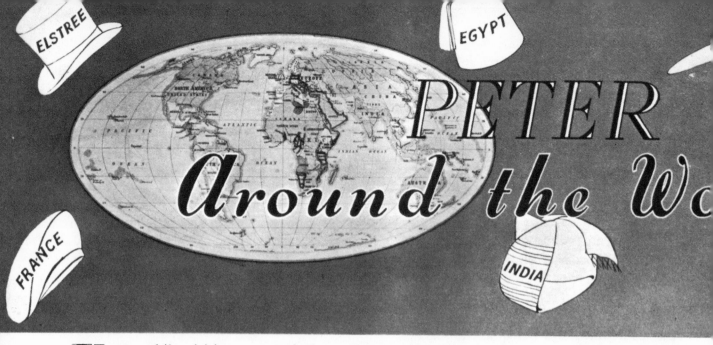

PETER
Around the Wo

IT was while visiting my mother one day, at the tender age of seven, that my trip to Hollywood began. Sir Thomas Paulson, M.P., had his office in the same building He was a friend of the family's and not infrequently I popped in to say " hello " or met him in the hall. On one of these occasions he asked me, " Young man, what are you going to be when you grow up ? " I told him, " I want to be a cinema star." I thought he'd never stop laughing. Good-naturedly he warned me " the General would skin you alive if he heard that." Reflecting for a few moments, I realized that Father, Sir Sidney, retired Lieutenant-General late of the Royal Fusiliers, probably would do just that—particularly if he thought I was serious. The army had been a tradition in our family, and actors—well, they're a jolly good bunch *BUT——* !

However, I knew Sir Thomas had interests in Elstree. I finally wangled his promise that I might have a pass to visit a studio and see what one of those marvellous places was like—" just for a lark." The pass from genial Sir Thomas cinched my ambitions, resulted in my getting my first part in a film, and eventually led to my coming to Hollywood !

When Mother took me to the studio I met Monty Banks and, as a result, fell into a part in " Poor Old Bill," the first of a series of " Old Bill " films in which I played. Father didn't " skin me alive " as Sir Thomas and I had anticipated, because he thought these films would get the acting bug out of my juvenile head. When it became apparent that I was becoming keener on the idea rather than cooling off it, the General decided that all of us should do some travelling. He was retired and could make the trips with us, so, naturally, Mother and I shared his enthusiasm to " see the world." Besides, the English law forbidding children

64

RALIA
TAHITI
HAWAII
AWFORD
ld to Hollywood
NEW ZEALAND
AMERICA

under fourteen to act in pictures had been passed and so my acting days were over at least for the moment.

Mother, Father and I were in Aix-les-Bains when I had my unfortunate accident. The villa we had there had a large, heavy glass door which I was in the habit of vigorously pushing open on my frequent and very swift comings and goings. One day the door stuck, and instead of flipping it open, my right hand went through the glass ! The arm was slashed from my wrist to the shoulder. Since then the hand has been somewhat of a handicap, despite my efforts to put it to work. I wouldn't mention these unpleasant details except that this childhood accident was destined to play a part in my coming to Hollywood.

While Mother and Dad and I travelled, and in between my lessons with an array of private tutors whose names would read like a United Nations' roll call, I took up every sport I could think of that might help overcome my handicap. I rode whenever I could beg, borrow or hire a horse ; learned to dance at Monte Carlo ; learned to play tennis in India (though I have to use my left hand for this) ; learned to swim in that lovely South Sea island paradise of Tahiti ; and took up surf-board riding at Waikiki Beach in Honolulu.

As a consequence, I've become more than usually keen on all sports and this is really an asset in films. I've never been able to manage golf, and I still have to write left-handed. Aside from that, I can truthfully say that my injury has never really stopped me from doing anything I wanted to except when the war broke out and I tried to enlist in the army. But I'm getting ahead of my story.

At home with his mother and father, M.G.M.'s Peter Lawford prevents a fast move from his mother in a game of cards ! Starting out from England, Peter went all over the world before reaching Hollywood.

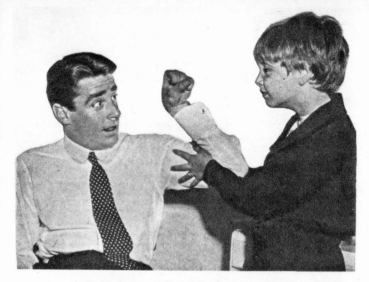

M.G.M. star " Butch " Jenkins inspects Peter's massive muscles in the dressing room. They played together in " My Brother Talks to Horses."

We had travelled from France to Egypt and India. From there we went down to Australia and New Zealand; then came Tahiti and Hawaii. After some more travelling, we finally landed in New York. The climate was cold there at the time, however, and the doctors suggested that sunny Southern California would be better for my ailing arm and hand. Well, as you know, California means Hollywood, and Hollywood means pictures. My early ambitions popped up again. Mother and Dad reminded me that I was in Hollywood for my health and not for another fling at the films. However, luck was with me and, while I won't bore you with the details, I landed a part at M.G.M. in " Lord Jeff " with Mickey Rooney and Freddie Bartholomew. This was a momentary triumph; war clouds were casting their shadows in Europe and Dad decided he should be back in England " just in case."

But when we got to New York and were about to embark for Europe, Hitler had beaten us to it and the war began. Mother and Dad still wanted to get back home, until friends persuaded them that Britannia could manage without one over-aged general, one charming mother and one adolescent son.

I think Dad would have insisted on our going anyway, except that the doctors urged I be taken to a warm climate, as my hand was acting up again. Dad decided that Florida would be the destination—he knew that if we went back to California I'd be trying to become an actor. So we went to Florida, with a side trip to Nassau in the Bahamas. My heart is warm for Nassau because it was there I found Spot, my faithful black and white dog, who, though a mongrel and now rather feeble, is still with us.

While we were in Florida monetary restrictions necessitated by the war entirely cut off Dad's income. Needless to say, this was a blow. Fortunately, I met a man in Miami, the city in which we were at the time, who had a large vacant area behind some shops he owned. Though I was still in my 'teens, he agreed to let me start an automobile parking lot in this space for a percentage of the earnings—despite my lack of years and business experience. I was very lucky. The parking lot enterprise not only kept the wolf from the door but enabled me to save what I thought then was quite a little money. In fact, I managed to save enough to come back to Hollywood and bring Mother and Dad, too.

Remembering my experience in " Lord Jeff," I figured that motion pictures would be more remunerative and more fun than the parking lot. I had just passed the age that would allow me to enlist in the army, but had been turned down because of my hand. So I figured that since military service was out, the next best thing was to see what I could do in films.

In Hollywood we managed to find an inexpensive apartment, and I started making the rounds of the studios. I never heard the word " no " so many times in my life ! In desperation I took a job ushering at the Westwood Village Theatre, a suburban cinema. The pay wasn't much but it was steady and enough to keep us eating.

Five months went by and I must have ushered tens of thousands of people to their seats. Just about the day I was promoted from an ordinary usher to ticket-taker, I got a surprise call from my film agent who said I must get out to M.G.M. immediately—" they're looking for a fellow for a part in ' Mrs. Miniver, " he said.

This was music to my ears, but a steady job is a steady job. I couldn't just walk out of the theatre. Fortunately, I was able to bribe a colleague to take my place. Then I hopped on a bus and got out to the studio. I not only got the job but was put to work on the spot, played the part, and got back to my ticket-taking before the theatre manager knew I was missing !

Well, that film part got me started in pictures again. After that the calls from the studios became more frequent and I played modest bits in " A Yank at Eton," " Thunderbirds," " Random Harvest " and " Mark Twain." Then came the *big* chance. I was called for and got the part of Irene Dunne's son in " The White Cliffs of Dover," and with this role came my contract with Metro-Goldwyn-Mayer. Since then I've been in " The Man From Down Under," " The Canterville Ghost," " Mrs. Parkington," " The Picture of Dorian Gray " and then " Son of Lassie."

It was while I was working in " The Picture of Dorian Gray " that Dad was finally " converted " from die-hard fusilier to enthusiastic actor ! He visited me on the set and they nabbed him for a part in the film. Since then he has become just as much of a film trouper as a military one. Between you and me, he's a good actor, too. And has he acquired the real trouper spirit ! Once when he was called to the studio for work, an old war wound started acting up in his knee. Despite the swelling and pain, he was determined to go to the studio. I went with him and acted as his " dresser." He was a good soldier and stuck it out until his chore was done, although he had to go to bed and have day and night nurses after the part was finished !

Since the " Lassie " film I've had really wonderful breaks in such films as " Cluny Brown," " My Brother Talks to Horses," " It Happened in Brooklyn," " Good News " and " On an Island with You."

" Easter Parade " with Fred Astaire and Judy Garland, and " Julia Misbehaves," starring Greer Garson and Walter Pidgeon, are my most recent two films. Working on the set of " Julia Misbehaves " was like " old home week " to me. There were many British actors in the cast. I always enjoy working with Miss Garson, and in addition to her there were Dame May Whitty who I think is " tops," as they say in America, Reginald Owen, Nigel Bruce, Elizabeth Taylor and a regiment of others. It may be some time before this film is released in England, but I know my friends " back home " will like it when it is.

Yes, I went the long way round to get to Hollywood, but I think many of the opportunities I have been given here can be attributed to my travel experiences. I've been lucky enough to jaunt all over the world but I think my big trip—the journey to ambition's end—has just begun !

" It's a cinch, nothing to it ! " says Peter Lawford as he skims across the water on skis during the location filming of M.G.M.'s " On an Island with You."

It's **DRAMA** not Glamour, for me !

says **Ann Blyth**

MAYBE most girls think of Hollywood as a splendid opportunity to be glamorous. The marvels that skilled make-up men can perform, the secret arts of the world's finest hair dressers, and the superb flattery of a wardrobe designed to dazzle, are a potent lure. Back up such a transformation with a striking background to match each mood, borrow such screen ammunition to intrigue the most dashing males, and you have Hollywood in a nutshell. Only that isn't what my chance to be in the movies meant to me at all!

In Universal-International's " Another Part of the Forest," Ann Blyth has a strong dramatic role opposite Fredric March. Ann says she prefers parts with " meat " in them, as opposed to glamorous roles.

Now that I'm nineteen I can look back at my five years in Hollywood with a veteran's shrewd eyes. Well, with almost that judicious a viewpoint. At least now I know I was right to go all out for strong dramatic roles in which I pulled no punches for sympathy, with nary a thought for how glamorous I could seem. Because I prefer to concentrate my pretending, focus it fully on actual scenes before a camera, and be absolutely relaxed the rest of the time, I haven't had to try to fit into a ravishing off-screen reputation. Which would be, I admit, a terrible strain on me.

Too much over-emphasis has been placed on the publicity build-up an aspiring actress needs, in my opinion. Certainly flashy stunts, elaborate posing as a beauty, and the mastery of fancy tricks to cause gasps, reap a lot of space and oral comment. But if that side of Hollywood just doesn't interest you, it can be skipped and with no hard feelings. I know this from my own experience.

When I received good notices for my performance in a Broadway hit at age fourteen, I expected it would be many a season before I'd be favoured by a bid from a studio. After eleven months in a New York theatre we took our play on a nine months' tour of all the major cities of America. (I still recall a command performance at the White House, followed by supper as a guest of President and Mrs. Roosevelt, as an unparalleled thrill.) We wound up at the Biltmore Theatre in Los Angeles and I was lucky enough to win my film contract because of my acting on the stage there.

My first four pictures were not right for me because I was cast as a formula *ingénue* When I asked for meatier roles nobody apparently heard me. But I didn't decide to " be seen " in black satin at Ciro's. I just quietly stuck to my own theory that all I lacked was a role jammed with heavy drama. When I was finally loaned out to enact Joan Crawford's rebellious daughter in " Mildred Pierce " I got back into my own stride. Since then I've been ruthlessly headstrong in most of my films, and that's given me all the emotion I want in my life.

I don't believe that I have earned the privilege of cutting capers. Again, what other people do is their own business. I want them to be equally tolerant of my own intentions. I want to live the life of a perfectly normal and, I hope, fairly bright girl. Eventually

I will fall in love and marry and run a home of my own. Until the big romance comes along I don't think I'm missing anything by my purposely uncomplicated routine.

I have at least a dozen things as " musts " to accomplish within the next few years. My professional goals include winning an Oscar for my acting and a dramatic regular radio show. Matrimony and motherhood lie not too far off, if I'm that fortunate and meet the right man. In the hobby department, I intend to play golf much better than I can now (I'm quite sad on the greens !) and I'm going to learn to fly. Speaking of travel, I visualize a trip around the world, with my longest stop-over in Ireland, where I have relatives I wish to visit leisurely. If I can somehow afford two sheer extravagances, I'll buy an expensive convertible car and a couple of race horses I can extravagantly enter at Santa Anita.

If you are worrying about my losing my head with the screen success I have dreams of attaining, please be reassured. I'm actually about the most conservative girl I know. When I got my first apartment in Hollywood, along with my introduction to studio life, I stayed in it until just a few months ago. I waited five years, until I'd saved enough money to buy a modest house, before moving up the scale a little. And I've just purchased my first mink coat, a symbol of financial progress, too. I stick to a strict budget, save a definite portion of my salary before I buy any luxuries.

When I finished one of the most difficult parts I have played—that of Regina in "Another Part of the Forest" with Fredric March, Dan Duryea and Florence Eldridge —and it met with the approval of Universal-International executives, I felt sure drama served more than glamour to further my career. Lillian Hellman, who wrote the original story, used the same characters in it, only in an earlier period, that she brought to life in " The Little Foxes." I focused my attention on the way the character should be played without even letting myself think of how Bette Davis played Regina as an older person in the film version of " The Little Foxes." Most of you will remember her exciting performance. I worked out my own characterization with the help of Director Michael Gordon, and between us I started work with a very definite idea of Regina and her vixenish personality.

Now I have been given a change from " hussy " parts as the amusingly fantastic sea-lady in " Mr. Peabody and the Mermaid "—a role that fires my imagination. The scaly tail which I have to wear as a mermaid encased me from the waist down in sixty pounds of buckshot besides the sponge rubber. I've dyed my hair for the first time—a reddish blonde. I got to keeping house temporarily in a mermaid's castle, submerged in beautiful, crystal blue water. For a very brief while I wondered if there mightn't be some fun in the glamour game !

Ann Blyth prefers roles that some actresses call " heavy "—but even she likes to relax occasionally, as here with William Powell in " Mr. Peabody and the Mermaid."

70

I'm an Artist – by Accident

Old China.

Medieval period.

says MEL ARCHER

MY work is called " scenario illustrating." It is extremely interesting. I stumbled onto it purely by accident and without any previous training to fit me for it.

I was born in Spokane, Washington ; we lived back to back with Bing Crosby, then known as Harry Lillis Crosby, and all went to school there, but Bing was just a little ahead of me.

Not one in a thousand would take me to be an artist—people are more likely to think I'm a plumber or a carpenter. I am over six feet, built like a wrestler, and my hands are large, practical-looking affairs—nothing long, tapering or sensitive-looking about them. I've lived and worked in oil fields. I've seen men killed there, and I've really roughed it . . . I've gone underground to cut off fires, they called us " rats." I've worked in lumber camps . . . all my life I've worked with my hands and brawn. I was a swimmer at seventeen, went to Amsterdam, Holland on the Olympic Team. I saw that wouldn't make me a living. My folks were poor—I wanted to help myself and them—so I decided to box. I made quite a little money in the fight ring.

All this was a strange but fertile background for an artist—suddenly I found myself drawing pictures. At night, after work on the oil fields, I'd sit just doodling with a pencil. Maybe it was the blood of my forefathers coming out in me. My father, his father before him, his grandfather and all his ancestors were tapestry weavers in England, where they were all born. I was the first of the Archer family to be born in America. My mother died when I was a child, I never knew my father. I was brought up by my grandfather.

People who saw the drawings which I'd made at night after work—mostly artists, writers, etc.—encouraged me to exhibit them. At Laguna Beach, a community about sixty-five miles south of Hollywood, I was given the opportunity to exhibit many of my Chinese characters, hoboes I'd painted, labourers, lumberjacks—just people of everyday life. I've never had even an hour's training as an artist or draughtsman, but after all these years I'm going to art school ; there are certain things I feel I must learn.

The work that I'm doing now was first established about ten years ago during the filming

Deep Congo.

Saracen period.

of " Marco Polo " at Goldwyn Studios. They were having trouble at that time with the make-up of the Chinese characters. (I had spent a year practising make-up when I worked with Max Factor, pioneer Hollywood make-up man, and Jim Barker from England, one of the best make-up men of all time.) I made sketches of how I envisioned the characters should look—a sort of basic design for make-up. Perc Westmore, make-up expert, saw them and asked me to work with him. He saw the possibilities of this type of thing and I've been with him ever since.

Warner Bros. is the only studio in the entire business which has such an extensive make-up department and employs an artist to do my type of work. It is also the only studio to have perfected the technique of taking life masks with the eyes open.

Make-up is done from basic plans, similar to blueprints used in building. Sketches are drawn, life masks made, make-up worked out. In making sketches we give the producer something to discuss. If he doesn't like it, we make changes. I make four drawings of an actor. The producer wants to see the man his way, the make-up man wants it another way. After a decision is reached I draw it that way. We combine the talents of the artist, make-up man, producer and director. We attempt to retain the actor's identity, yet resemble the character he is supposed to portray.

In order to do these drawings a knowledge of anatomy is important—square blocks won't fit in round holes—I have to know anatomy so I'll know where the lines come when the character ages. Proportion is important. I never put a tall head-dress on a tall girl's head. Her hair has to be arranged to balance her height. I have to combine the functions of both painter and sculptor.

In " The Adventures of Don Juan " Westmore deviated from the period to this extent : the time is one demanding cavalier wigs, when the men wore their hair down to their shoulders ; but because of the beautiful costumes of the period worn by both men and women in the picture, he kept the men in semi-short *modern* hair so that in the close-ups the men won't look like girls.

When it came to the ladies, he attempted to enact the period, but also kept a modern feeling so it is pleasing and could, in fact, be an ordinary hair style.

Here is something else I learned from Perc Westmore that might interest the ladies : in colour pictures the make-up must be applied as thinly as possible. The reason for this is that colour when projected is magnified. Being magnified, it intensifies itself— in other words, the cheek and lip rouge would be less than the amount you would use on the street, and very pale ; because of the magnification intensifying it, it is brought up to natural colour. No blacks are used—no lines around the eyes, etc.—no green eye shadows, no blue eye shadows, only browns and greys. For example, we have a player, such as Alan Hale, who is ruddy in complexion. Make-up applied on him will be on the yellow side or ochre side—very thin—the ruddiness coming through, blending with the yellow make-up, giving even skin tone. If we did not do this he would be red as fire on the screen. The matter of blending colour, line, highlight and shadow work is done very subtly—we must have perfect blending, no line of demarcation. We do, for musicals, accentuate the make-up

72

Deep Congo.

Old China.

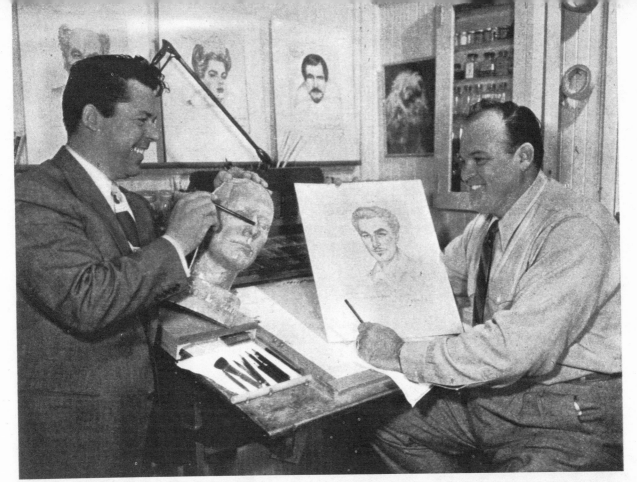

Mel Archer, Warner Bros.' scenario illustrator, with Perc Westmore famous make-up chief.

Below, an Archer sketch of Errol Flynn, as he will appear in " The Adventures of Don Juan."

for a line of showgirls—we will go a little overboard to get over the feeling of the theatrical; but in dramatic pictures we keep them just as natural as possible.

To get back to the scenario illustrating which I am doing at Warner Bros.' Studio, it gives any artist the greatest background for painting, inasmuch as you are dealing constantly with living people. It was a pleasure to draw Ann Sheridan—she has so much animation and such definite features. Errol Flynn is fine to work with. Bette Davis has an unusual face—she has so much emotion and hidden depth in her features . . . she is beautiful in an odd way; she's not just a cover girl. She has fire and depth.

Yes, indeed, my spot here at Warner Bros. is an enviable one—any artist would give the world to have such an interesting array of models.

73

HOLLYWOOD

Right : Dramatic black flowers trim the neckline of Audrey Totter's black crepe dress, which can be worn on or off the shoulder.

Ava Gardner, M.G.M. star, in a field of golden grain, wearing a popular type of California playsuit.

FASHION PARADE

Left : These ultra sophisticated lounging pyjamas were designed for Ginger Rogers in Columbia's " It Had to be You." They are of black pebble crepe, highlighted with sequins with appliqué work of American beauty roses on the left shoulder and hip. Notice the new plunge neckline and low cut arm holes.

Linda Darnell wearing one of her famous miniatures. She likes old-fashioned jewellery. 20th Century-Fox consider her one of their top stars.

Ellen Drew models a white brocade with four leaf clover design in gold thread; the strapless bodice is held by cleverly devised draping. The skirt is finely pleated and very full. Ellen stars in Columbia's " The Man from Colorado " with Glenn Ford.

A study in bronze slipper satin—dinner suit worn by Janis Paige, star of Warner Bros.' Technicolor release, "Romance on the High Seas," a Michael Curtiz production. It has tailored jacket embroidered in bronze and gold sequins and bugle beads, pencil slim skirt slit almost knee-high. Gloves and stole to match.

Left : Lovely Dorothy McGuire, one of Hollywood's finest actresses, looks especially charming in simple clothes like this pale blue crepe de chine tucked blouse. Her double row of pearls give a smart finish to the neck-line.

Above : M.G.M.'s Frances Gifford achieves new heights of glamour with this hat made of two luscious black roses on a white straw sailor entwined with black net.

Right : the woman in white is Eleanor Parker, Warner Bros.' star of the forthcoming production, " The Woman in White." Miss Parker will next be seen in " The Voice of the Turtle," film version of the popular stage success.

Left : Susan Hayward models an ensemble designed in navy wool ; the cape-back jacket buttons on to the slim skirt with three huge buttons at the front. The tailored white crepe blouse with tucked front is fastened with Susan's emerald and gold studs.

Left : Valli, another of David O. Selznick's stars, who makes her debut in " The Paradine Case," here models a lovely evening gown that will be the envy of all feminine readers. The frill top enhances the marble smoothness of her lovely back and shoulders.

Here's an idea for those keen on knitting to copy : 19-year-old Ann Blyth, who made a star appearance in " Mildred Pierce," wears an unusual sweater, composed of white knitted base and a yoke of saxe-blue material. Ann is a Universal-International star.

Lois Maxwell, talented young Canadian actress who makes her screen debut in Warner Bros.' "That Hagen Girl," likes Tina Lesser's shirred wool printed blouse and apron ensemble. She uses the ascot tie to tie back her golden locks. Full circular skirt is of tomato red gaberdine.

Above : This neat outfit worn by Columbia's Gloria Henry is made of wool, and the colour scheme is grey with red and green stripes. The flannel blouse and pirate stocking cap with long tassel are bright red.

Above : " Dotty " is the name of this stunning spring hat designed for Dorothy Hart. The soaring brim of soft blue felt shows a fanciful array of yellow and purple pansies and darker blue veiling.

Stars off Duty

Above : While making " My Own True Love " on the Paramount lot, beautiful Phyllis Calvert found time to drop in for a visit to Bob Hope while he was making " The Pale Face."

Top right : Warner Bros.' star Alexis Smith is a horse fancier who was in her glory when she appeared with Ronald Reagan in " Stallion Road," in the role of a trainer of thorough-bred stallions.

Right : Rosalind Russell, who caps a career of superb performances with her great part in " Mourning Becomes Electra," is caught relaxing in her flower-filled garden.

Above : Mickey Rooney planned to take Sam Levene's photograph, but he forgot to put a film in the camera ! They are clowning on the set of "Killer McCoy."

Above : In real life Mr. and Mrs. Hodiak, Anne Baxter and John Hodiak, examine some stills from the picture they are doing together—M.G.M.'s "Homecoming."

Warner Bros.' star Ronald Reagan, who will be seen with the Swedish actress Viveca Lindfors, in "Night Unto Night." He is shown here on his favourite mare "Tar Baby."

Right : No, it isn't Sherlock Holmes. Look again. It's Robert Taylor fooling with Audrey Totter on the set of "High Wall."

Above : It looks as if Vic Mature is dating some lucky girl. Dog lovers will say there is more than one handsome person in this picture.

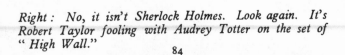

Even dynamic Danny Kaye relaxes once in a while—before rushing on with his next piece of inspired fooling, which will be Samuel Goldwyn's " A Song is Born."

Macdonald Carey—Paramount featured player and his wife Betty, suffering the reverse of the nationwide housing problem. They have a beautiful Hollywood home—but only a few sticks of furniture.

English actor Robert Douglas, now under contract to Warner Bros., in the garden of his newly acquired Pacific Palisades home with his wife, Suzanne. His American screen debut is opposite Alexis Smith in " The Decision of Christopher Blake."

Above : Joan Fontaine's favourite hobby, which she shares with her mother, is working in a greenhouse.
Below : Who wouldn't be a Scotty, when you can get all that attention from Barbara Stanwyck and Van Heflin.

The clue to this star's identity lies in the two letters at the foot of the sketch—F.S. You're right, it is Frank Sinatra.

Strolling arm in arm one day were Mr. and Mrs. John Agar (Shirley Temple to you), when who should pop up but the camera-man, so. . . .

George Montgomery plays with his collie pal " Cap." He is married to singing actress Dinah Shore.

" Look ! No hands ! " Red Skelton shows off in an effort to entice Virginia O'Brien on to the saddle of his tandem, in M.G.M.'s " Merton of the Movies."

Two of the screens loveliest blondes are caught by the candid camera on the set of Paramount's " The Sainted Sisters." Lady with the veil is Veronica Lake. Midway is William Demarest. Halfway through a mug of coffee is Joan Caulfield.

Jack Carson beats out a few bars of rhythm on the studio piano as he rehearses a song he will sing in the forthcoming Technicolor musical, Warner Bros.' " Two Texas Knights," co-starring Dennis Morgan.

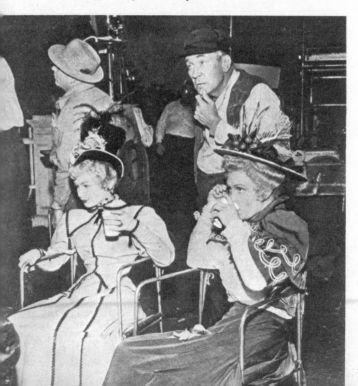

It is not an unusual sight around Paramount to see Bob Hope and Bing Crosby dressed up in the uniforms of two of America's most famous baseball clubs, in which they have financial interests.

"VARIETY is the spice of my life" — LORETTA YOUNG

WHEN I was five years old, I started my film career—in practically invisible roles. I was either one of a number of children dancing around a maypole, or a youngster in a schoolroom. But at twelve, I got a chance to play a real role. My sister Polly Ann had been called for a part, but was ill, so I dressed up and went in her place. The director demanded perfection and his sarcasm was too much for me. I got upset and went home. Then I thought it over and decided nothing could be gained by running away from things—so I went back.

From then on, I realized that fear, losing one's temper, or becoming dictatorial with the first blush of success is not to be tolerated.

After playing too many similar roles and finding one's self falling into an expected pattern, it seemed to me time to determine to change one's type to avoid becoming absolutely stereotyped. Before I felt I was prepared for diversified roles, I had played innumerable " glamorous " girls. Playing just a pretty girl in so many films had become monotonous. But I was supposed to be a trouper, so I played them, and other so-called " glamour roles " until seven years of rushing from one part into another had so taxed my enthusiasm and strength it was impossible to keep it up. I took stock and felt I had served enough of an apprenticeship to be capable of selecting my pictures. Three pictures a year seemed enough. Next, if I were to achieve real stature as an actress, I needed stories that would give me a variety of parts. I changed my career pattern.

So more recently, I have had variety. I played a trusting New England bride in " The Stranger "—if you remember the picture, I was deceived by an arch-villain husband, played by Orson Welles. I enjoyed every minute of work on the picture. In " The Perfect Marriage," I enjoyed playing a smart up-to-date New York woman—a fashion editor. Then the script of " The Farmer's Daughter " was handed me by Dore Schary and the role of Katie permitted a real characterization. It was quite a bit of variety to play the farm girl, wearing the simple clothes, coarse stockings and rough shoes of an out-of-doors worker, to milk cows, to feed chickens. It was fascinating to understand this girl who knew so well the hard side of life and had a first-hand appreciation of the problems of farm people. I loved Katie—she was such a real and literally down-to-earth person.

Next came " The Bishop's Wife." When Samuel Goldwyn asked me to read this script I thought, here is a fine story and a part it would be a joy to play. So I said, " Yes, indeed, I should be delighted to play the part of Julia." And it was a delightful engagement. David Niven played the Bishop and Cary Grant was the angel who came to earth

In her early films Loretta Young did not always get the variety she craves for. But she enjoyed playing in "Ramona," in "Cafe Metropole" with Tyrone Power, and in "Zoo in Budapest."

and brought much brightness and vivacity and warmth not only into Julia's staid existence but the lives of all surrounding her and her Bishop. We started work on the picture. After almost three weeks' shooting, Mr. Goldwyn, the producer—and a glorious perfectionist—decided the script should be re-written! He assigned Robert Sherwood and Leonardo Bercovici to do the work. The result was an entirely new and different film. Not a foot of the first start was kept. It was a costly decision for Mr. Goldwyn, but a wise and right one. We who played in "The Bishop's Wife" felt that those who saw it could not help but leave the theatre with a feeling that it is possible to live happily, harmoniously and progressively if we will listen to that still, small voice—our real angel. However, in the picture Cary Grant was anything but a still, small voice—he was a vibrant and articulate angel. One whose words and deeds spread happiness and progress through the lives of all he met—and blessed—in a most enchanting fashion!

After making the decision to play in "The Bishop's Wife," I was gratified that my belief in the part was shared by many. It was shown in England at the Command Performance and I had the great pleasure of being in London again.

It was fortunate that I had just finished my part in "Rachel and The Stranger" for R.K.O. when the invitation came to me to attend the Command Performance showing of "The Bishop's Wife," so no production schedule prevented my acceptance. It was an unforgettable and important experience. I learned so much from the magnificent manner in which England met its austerity programme and it was a thrilling experience to be presented to the King and Queen.

"Rachel and The Stranger" is the story of Rachel, a bondswoman, and is laid in the early nineteenth century in what was *then* called the Northwest—Western Pennsylvania or Eastern Ohio. Actually, we made the film in the glorious Oregon woods. This role was my most severe departure from glamour. As Rachel, I wore one outfit, an ill-fitting dress of roughest homespun and heavy, clumsy shoes. My hair, uncurled, was brushed back, with unruly wisps—as became a woman who laboured, as women did in those days, making a home in the wilderness. It was her strong character which made her worthwhile. In the script, it took a little dog, played by Corky, to start Rachel toward a happy ending. Because of the dog's affection for Rachel, the dog's young master, her stepson by virtue of her marriage-in-name only, and his father, to whom Rachel was bonded, felt there must be some good in her. The story unfolds with many exciting scenes. Indians burn down the family's log cabin—and the gay romancing of tall, dark stranger Robert Mitchum gives Rachel's master and husband, played by William Holden, his first incentive to notice her as a woman. It is a strong, stark story charmingly told against a rugged background of great beauty. Rachel is a far cry from the glamorous creatures I played for so many years, until I rebelled. Being typed is being in a sort of prison—I suppose if I had been typed in stark character parts, I would never have been happy until I had tried the glamorous roles! Variety is necessary to all of us and any actress who wants to grow in her career should play every and any sort of part to which she is physically adapted.

The new objective in my professional life was exciting and ensured constant enjoyment of my continuing career. And limiting the number of pictures gives me the time I want and need to devote to my growing family and my husband and our home. No matter how much help one has, there is no substitute for a mother's ruling hand. Unforeseen circumstances can change any family's fortune, so I believe in the importance of bringing up our children to be self-reliant and fitted to meet any adversity.

My mother's early discipline and training taught me and my sisters to manage for ourselves. With four girls in the house, she had to insist upon a sense of order. All of my sisters have had screen careers—Polly Ann was the first to become an actress; she retired when she married Carter Herman, Los Angeles business man. Betty (known on the screen as Sally Blane) is married to Norman Foster, the director (he directed " Rachel and The Stranger "). And my youngest sister, Georgiana, is married to the handsome Ricardo Montalban, who is such a fine young actor with an excitingly successful career ahead of him, I'm sure.

At home, I was called Gretch—and still answer to it, as my real name was (and still is) Gretchen. When at thirteen I embarked on my " adult " screen career in " Naughty But Nice," Colleen Moore suggested I be given the

In " Rachel and The Stranger," Loretta Young plays the role of Bill Holden's pioneer wife. The role is a big departure from her previous glamorous assignments, and recalls her excellent performance in " The Farmer's Daughter."

93

name of Loretta; but I never knew why she picked that particular one until years later, when Colleen visited the set of " The Farmer's Daughter." It was then she told me that she had named me after the princess in a beloved fairy tale. I have always liked the name which became mine not long after I so impetuously reported for work in Polly Ann's place.

In the early days of my career, I was a Wampas " Baby Star " after I was given, at the age of fourteen, the feminine role in " Laugh, Clown, Laugh " with Lon Chaney. The Wampas—a group of Hollywood publicity men—has passed out of existence but they were active long enough to start many of us on our way. I was grateful to bridge the gap between silent and talking pictures without losing ground in my career. I was fortunate to pass the speaking tests when so many promising young players were dropped. I have never forgotten that it must have been heartbreaking for them.

Among my early pictures, I liked " Ramona," which I did with Don Ameche as Alessandro. I liked the charm of " Zoo in Budapest " with Gene Raymond, and in " Cafe Metropole " I must have been the envy of many girls, for Tyrone Power was my leading man. In " The Men in Her Life," I played a ballerina and loved it despite the hours and hours of gruelling practice.

I hope I am fortunate enough to continue to find parts that are diversified, in good pictures. I am interested first in making good pictures and would rather have a lesser part in a fine picture than all the scenes in a mediocre one. And I hope such good pictures will continue to give me the spice of variety which keeps every actress happy and on her toes.

Against the wonderful panorama of the Oregon backwoods, Bill Holden begins to realize the merit of his bondswoman wife, as enacted by Loretta Young.

Just an Inventor at Heart

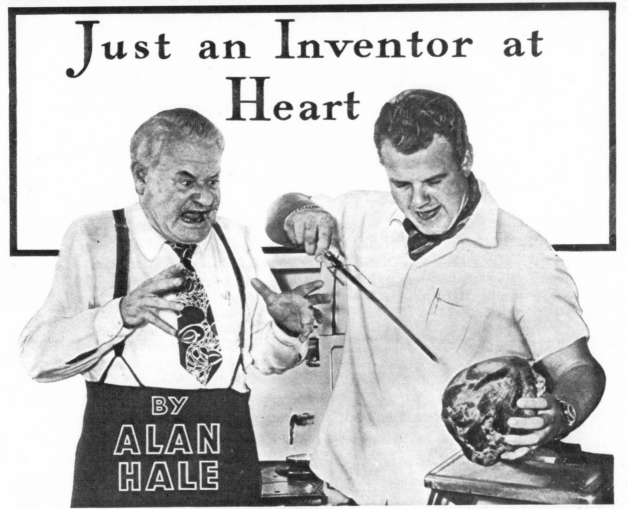

BY ALAN HALE

THOUGH for thirty years I have paid most of my attention to the theatre and the stage, I have always managed to take time out to be interested in the other fellow's and my own inventions. I don't build things myself: I conceive the idea and call in an engineer to work it out, or I pass on the ideas to someone who thinks along the same line and has the time to complete it. In fact, I formed a company, Alan Hale Enterprises, to take care of this sort of business.

For a long while I felt that glasses were cumbersome, that they obscured sight on both sides. So we put on the market a pair of glasses that have no nose pad, the lenses being held above by a clip which continues back and behind the ears. Vision is not obscured at any point.

Invention is simply a short cut to a function, and if you have something that does what others have been doing and does them easier, you have added something new to the art.

We re-engineered moving picture seats, the kind that slide back so people can pass without those seated jumping up. We had corps of engineers taking out " the bugs "— meaning defects in an inventor's lingo. Then we got them down to being noiseless. When they became practical we put them on the market, and we are now selling them all over the world.

Even in my college days I thought the best ideas were those involving safety factors.

We have re-engineered four-wheeled brakes, food products, easy chairs. Since we established our business many people have sent in for consideration things that are just contraptions—games, useless things. I have a mind agreeable to invention and an appreciation of really good ideas, and now I am able to do something about it. Debussy said you could appreciate a beautiful sunset, but you couldn't create one. Some of the boys on the lot of Warner Bros. have had very good ideas with which I've helped with my knowledge of patent law, and so forth—some of them are doing pretty well.

Invention is a strange thing. You can get about one good one—one fair one, really—out of two thousand. Then something will come along like the fellow who is supposed to have invented the top. He started to make them and it grew and grew—or like the fellow who got the idea of putting kindling wood into bundles. Few things are actually invented—it is just a matter of function put together.

Alan Hale records his son's bass voice on a machine. . . . " Not my invention—wish it were," says Hale, " It's a wonder."

Of course, some of the things that have been invented aren't so functional, and objections have been raised to them. In some countries in Europe—in England, for example—you may get a summons for blowing your horn after dusk unless you have a good reason for it. In Prague they don't allow horns, and it's been proven that this has reduced accidents, in some instances as much as sixty per cent—not so many jangled nerves when there are no horns. I had an idea—still have it, as a matter of fact—whereby you can't blow your horn unless your foot is on the brake pedal. If you should have to blow your horn, you should be in a position to stop if the horn-blowing doesn't rid you of what's in your way. Now there's an invention for open road driving that controls bright lights without the foot pedal. If you're coming towards me, my headlights will dim yours and your headlights will dim mine. It's a violation in America not to dim your headlights when passing a car, and this ensures complying with the law.

I personally think that some day they will have an arrangement where your radio won't disturb you when you're in your car. You're so concerned with what you're hearing, it dulls your other senses. They tell the story of a driver who was listening to " Information Please." The programme told its listeners to close their eyes for five seconds and a certain thing would take place. The fellow driving the car closed his eyes and ran into something ahead of him. Something certainly took place in that instance.

America is a push-button country : you press a button to wash clothes, open doors, light the stove, take care of the baby, and now there is a sound receiver which can be put on a cradle. If the baby cries, it will rock the cradle.

I have a system, hit upon when we were fiddling around trying to stop motor noise coming through the radio : it is completely detached from the radio (U.S.A. Federal Communications Commission does not permit anything to be attached to the radio in your car). We built a separate speaker and separate mike—it's directional so that you speak only towards parked cars at the sidewalk. At first I rigged it as a two-way, but that was too noisy and picked up all the street noises and those of all other cars. One of the funniest incidents with that system took place when I rolled up behind a fellow I knew, at about 4.30 one Sunday. He was walking along the street, and I had the Jack Benny programme on the radio and projected it through the speaker. Each time there was a lull in the programme I would say, " Rotten, isn't it ? " This fellow didn't know where it was coming from because all the sounds came through the same speaker. I've had fun with the police and in parking stations. I finally had to put a lock on it in parking lots as the attendants would get in and play it so long, it ran down the battery. I had one of these systems put on John Charles Thomas' car—he is like a big kid, always using it.

I created this originally with the thought that it could be used in the army on training fields. A commanding officer could go out on the field and direct his conversation to a good one-eighth or one-quarter mile.

Alan Hale astride his specially designed motorcycle, compares notes with Dennis Morgan on the Warner's lot.

My company, besides making theatre seats and other things, put out a potato chip maker which allows the use of any size potato for making chips or wafers. Since we've been in the dither about critical materials, inability to get priorities, we have let most things ride. Now that manufacturing is coming to the fore again, we may start on other things, and from that things will grow. Ours is a closed corporation.

The average inventor always feels that his products are worth a million dollars—or

" Watch the birdie." Alan Hale, Jnr. has his father as a patient sitter in this outdoor portrait.

wants 51 per cent of the stock—or wants to be chairman of the company—or wants to have it named after him. He has no idea of a financial goal. If a man builds something, he must have some idea of what he wants to make out of it.

Many people think if you send a patent in, it will be stolen. That's not true. Most manufacturers do not want to spend money in court, and do not want to steal anything. They are perfectly willing to pay for it.

We are holding many patents at present, apart from the theatre seats. I doubt very much if we will attempt anything on a large scale until almost the end of 1948. All things being equal, unless I am tied up on pictures, I am going to try to get over to Sweden— there are two or three things I've seen there that we are interested in and we have some things they want — then I will come down through England.

To-day, the outstanding country, so far as invention is concerned, is America—for the number of inventions.

The wheel was the greatest contribution of all time to mechanics. It is the one thing never made by Nature. Everything in Nature is more or less controlled by virtue of a torque set-up, the same as a conch shell. We are at 23/1 2 degrees to the pole star and we have a mutation which is a wobble—that's why there could not be anything actually round in Nature.

At one time I thought that I would like to go into chemistry, but in my capacity as an actor I wasn't in one place long enough; and when I first went into business I didn't have money enough. But I've worked a lot in chemistry. My father was a chemist. I dabbled in it a lot in my workshop at home, but my son, Alan, Jnr., took up photography and turned it into a dark room—but I still manage to keep a vice and a few tools around.

It is only of late I have been in a position to take a practical interest in inventions. As a young man I had been in the theatre, then did pictures—I worked during summer vacation while going to college in 1909 in Philadelphia. The following year I went down with the Orpheum Stock Company in Philadelphia; then the following year I went to New York on the stage. In the New York play we were all so good, it lasted only two weeks. I have been in pictures longer than on the stage—in fact, have been in and out of them for thirty-eight years. My interest in inventions goes back to when I was seventeen, but it would have taken too much money to promote them in those days. I just didn't have it—now I'm in a position to afford the inventions and can also enjoy my movie work.

All of which is to prove that as an actor, I'm a pretty good inventor—or is it vice versa ?

Answers Inc.

IRENE DUNNE

QUITE recently and more or less by accident, I got into the business of trying to settle people's problems. It's strictly a no-pay job, but it's so fascinating that I have difficulty finding time for my usual hobbies, and sometimes I wonder if it isn't likely to impinge on time which should be devoted to my job—except that if that should happen, I'd have to go out of the answer business (because very few people would tell me about their problems if I weren't an actress).

A strange phenomenon occurs when a person becomes a star in Hollywood. A large part of the public automatically assumes that stardom makes a person an oracle on all manners of topics, from international affairs to how to win back a wandering husband.

The American press quite frequently subscribes to this theory, too.

It was shortly after "Cimarron" was released that I first became aware of this situation. A newspaper reporter asked if I thought the American " bank holiday " of 1933 would end the depression.

At that time, I was still pretty innocent about publicity and kindred topics and declared that, even if I had formulated an opinion, I would not consider it proper to express it.

But, proving how insidious such flattery is, recently I undertook to answer each month, via "Silver Screen," a popular American fan magazine, any question or problem any man, woman, or child wished to write me about.

This, undoubtedly, was very brash of me but, nevertheless, in my own defence, I must declare that I do not undertake the answers lightly ; that I really *am*

A scene from " I Remember Mama," in which Irene Dunne plays with Philip Dorn. It is a story of the ups and downs of family life. Barbara Bel Geddes (right) has an important role.

concerned and interested in these questions and problems and discuss the serious ones with my friends and my own counsellors before setting down my opinions.

The " answer job " came about this way. Lester Grady, the editor of " Silver Screen," was interviewing me on the set of " Life With Father." We got into a discussion of fan mail. I told him of some letters which had been stimulating, or even inspiring to me. (These are the unusual, of course. Most fan letters simply ask for an autographed picture.) And I told him, too, of how often fans, in their letters, related their worries and asked for advice.

Mr. Grady suggested then that I reply to " typical problems " through the medium of his magazine. The " problem letters " are sent to the magazine and then relayed to me. With the help of two secretaries, I read them all. We choose particularly typical or particularly interesting letters to answer in the magazine beneath a—usually shortened— copy of the letter. I cannot send personal replies to the writers and, of course, there are sometimes letters about problems which I could not possibly touch upon.

The largest number of letters come from teen-agers, and the majority of those want to know how to get into the movies, or how to become a singer. The next largest group come from girls with boy-friend trouble. Then a great many ask for advice on marital problems. The majority of these problems seem to be the result of hasty war-time marriages. A surprising number of men ask for advice in handling their " women "— wives or girl-friends. Quite a lot of girls ask for beauty advice, and there are some letters dealing with problems of etiquette. One girl, an orphan, asked whom she could have give her in marriage. (I had to go to the book of Etiquette, Emily Post, myself for advice on that one !)

Naturally, in answering many letters, I point out that my knowledge of the situation is necessarily sketchy—I write letters, not books—and so, in addition to giving general advice, I suggest the writer consult his doctor or his own religious counsellor depending upon the nature of the problem.

One such suggestion was made in the case of a widow who wrote that she had met, for the first time since child-hood, a first cousin, and had fallen in love with him. She wanted my advice as to whether they should marry.

Pointing out that, as a Catholic, marriage between first cousins was against my belief, I mentioned Dr. Joshua Loth Liebman, author of the best-selling (in the United States) book " Peace of Mind," had been happily married to his first cousin for nineteen years, and that there had been numerous historic instances of marriages between first cousins. My advice

Irene Dunne spends a great deal of time answering letters addressed to her, and trying to settle people's personal problems.

was that she discuss her situation with her family doctor and also her religious adviser.

A man wrote that he had loved a woman for six years but could never get up the courage to ask her to marry him. Taking Robert Browning as an example, I suggested he write the lady, just as he had me, telling her how he felt about her and, for good measure, advised he send the lady flowers along with the *billet-doux*.

A young woman wrote that her husband, an ex-GI, was attending college and that, while he had thought her beautiful when he was in the Army, now constantly compared her disparagingly with co-eds.

Director Michael Curtiz arranges his cast for "Life With Father." William Powell plays the head of the family, Jimmy Lydon his eldest son, and Irene Dunne his lovable, scatter-brained wife.

" First, he asked me to bleach my hair," she wrote. " I did that; a few weeks later, he told me to henna it. I discovered that each time he had told me to change the colour or style of my hair, or suggested I wear different kinds of co-ed clothes, he had developed a crush on a new girl and was trying to re-make me like her."

Stating that her husband's behaviour indicated that he was either fickle or very young, the answer advised that she stop switching her hair colour to suit her husband's whim—for the hair's sake if nothing else—and to study her type, analyze her assets and faults, and try to develop a genuine personality of her own. It also suggested that she consider studying selected courses and pointed out that, for the most part, collegians wore casual, attractive clothes which might well suit her. The reply concluded : " If his fickleness continues over a period of years, you will, of course, have a more serious problem to meet."

Not at all unusual was a letter from a woman asking how to augment her family's income. Her only talent, she said, was for knitting wool socks. I'd never heard of the town she wrote from ; in fact, I couldn't find it on my map, but finally ascertained from the Automobile Club that it was a village located about forty miles from a sizable town. The answer advised her to market her socks through men's stores in that city.

A nineteen-year-old girl in Brooklyn wrote that she loved S . . . , a young man of twenty-two, who declared he did not want to marry until he was thirty. She and his parents thought S . . . was " afraid of getting married."

Suggesting that she and the young man's parents were " pressuring " S . . . on the subject of marriage, I advised her to continue having dates with the young man, and to be as attractive as possible.

Only rarely do I learn if my advice has been followed, or the results, but five months later she wrote that she had married the erstwhile reluctant young man, and that they were divinely happy.

Irene Dunne with her screen son, Steven Brown, waits at the hospital during a critical moment in R.K.O.'s " I Remember Mama."

If only I could be as decisive and dispassionate about my own problems!

GET IN THERE AND SWIM !

JOHNNY WEISSMULLER

FOR the past fifteen years I've been making a pretty good living out of swinging from trees into jungle rivers, swimming across the river, and swinging back up into the trees. A lot of words have been written about " Tarzan," but practically nothing has been said, during all these years, of the man who made " Tarzan " possible—or, at least, made it possible for me to play him on the screen. I'm going to rectify that situation right now.

Back around 1922 I was going to school at Lane Technical High School in Chicago, and working afternoons and evenings as an elevator boy at the Illinois Athletic Club. The club had a swimming instructor who, even then, had been there so many years that no one could remember just when he had been hired.

In those days, the swimming pool was closed at 9 p.m. and the coach went home. The elevators were shut off at 9.30 p.m. and I went home—supposedly. The truth was, however, that every night, when I'd go down to the locker room to change from my operator's uniform to street clothes, I'd sneak through a glass partition into the pool room and take myself a nice dip in one of the finest swimming pools in the U.S.A. This was strictly against all club rules, for the lights were out and if anyone should have trouble in the water after the nine o'clock deadline, the fact wouldn't be known until nine o'clock the next morning—and that would be a little late for a drowning man.

This went on for several months without any trouble, and I thought I was becoming a terrific swimmer. Then one night, just as I was in the centre of the pool, the world came down upon me, in the form of lights coming on around me. One minute the room was pitch dark, the next, it looked like the Great White Way. And on the side of the pool stood what looked to me like the biggest man I'd ever seen.

It was William Bachrach, coach of the Illinois Athletic Club of Chicago, Illinois, largest athletic club in the United States—in which I was an elevator operator. And I was in the middle of his domain, the swimming pool—and he was roaring!

" Who are you ? " says the same thing, in nicer language, that he finally sputtered at me. " Get out of there this instant ! " was a continuation.

The room was warm, but I was cold and shivering as I finally climbed up the longest three-step ladder in the world (so it seemed to me) to the side of the pool, where he towered over me.

That was my introduction to the Man Who Made Tarzan Swim. I won't go into the horrible details of the next fifteen minutes—when he accused me vociferously of everything from house-breaking to attempted suicide—but after he had run down, he ordered me back into the pool.

" So you think you're a swimmer ? Okay . . . . swim ! "

I jumped in, raced the length of the pool and back again, and was positive I'd impressed him. That idea didn't last long.

" You're pretty bad," he snorted, " but I can make *anybody* a swimmer who wants to swim as badly as you apparently do. Report here to-morrow instead of the elevator."

The next afternoon I was back with Bachrach and he became my coach. He coached me until the sight of water would nauseate me. I wondered what I had ever seen in swimming. I couldn't even face a drinking glass without flinching.

" You wanted to swim, didn't you ? " Bill would shout. " Now swim ! "

Bill Bachrach has probably coached more famous swimmers than any other man alive—Jamison Handy, Oliver Horn, and dozens of others, and his attitude toward me was just what it had been toward all of them.

As I've said, he's an enormous man, and hardly ever gets in the water himself. But he can show you, from the side of the pool, more faults in five minutes than you can discover yourself in five years—and, what's more important, show you how to correct them.

By 1924 Bill had made me swim right onto the American Olympic team. Was he satisfied ? No. When the games were over and I came back to the Club a winner of my events, his first words were : " Get in the pool and I'll show you where you were wrong." He meant it, and he did it.

By 1930 I had come to California and was in the pool at the Hollywood Athletic Club. I felt lost because every time I'd look up at the side of the pool I'd expect to see Bachrach, and he was back in Chicago.

Another man stood watching me, though.

" How'd you like to go into pictures ? " he said.

" Doing what ? " I asked. " Swimming ? "

I thought Bachrach had sent him out here to spy on me, but it developed he was Cyril Hume, the novelist, and he was in the throes of writing a screen play called " Tarzan and the Ape Man." He had everything but Tarzan.

I called Bachrach long distance and told him about the offer. " Think I ought to do it ? " " Sure," he replied, " but get in plenty of practice before you even make a test—and call me just before you get in the pool."

Two days later I called Bill, followed his instructions as to what to do in front of the camera (Bachrach was used to newsreels) and got the job. I became Tarzan via Bachrach.

I Dressed a Queen
by Leah Rhodes

TWO years ago I was assigned to " The Adventures of Don Juan "—we planned to do it in black and white then. We have used for Technicolor some of the things that we started in black and white, but it's very rarely that this works out.

I was a little luckier than Hartnell in London who dressed Princess Elizabeth for her wedding, because I had two years in which to prepare myself to dress a queen. My queen is Viveca Lindfors, who plays Austrian born Queen Margaret, wife of Philip III. However, my job was a little more difficult in one way because it meant doing extensive research of the fashions of royal houses in the seventeenth century. In the costuming, we are not sticking too closely to the originals, but have made the costumes more dramatic for story purposes, since " The Adventures of Don Juan " is not purely an historical episode, but a fantasy. We have taken licence and treated Queen Margaret as an individual—a woman who would have her own individual tastes. After all, there must have been people in those days who were individual in their likes and dislikes about clothes.

Besides the queen, I had to dress a number of other ladies, women beloved by Don Juan and the ladies-in-waiting to the queen. I had to dress them carefully in order to indicate the different types that intrigued the gay international philanderer. They were dressed in colours and styles suited to their individual personalities.

I like to take my inspiration from the paintings of great masters. For this picture I studied Velasquez more than any other painter. Most of the great masters emphasized certain things in their clothes. I also studied Rembrandt for collars. We were able to take licence in a way, for at that time styles were being brought to the Spanish courts from all the countries and we had a lot of leeway in our choice. Spain at the time was the dominating country of the Continent, and at her courts visitors from Holland, Italy, and Austria were received.

Clothes for this movie were designed for movement, for action. Colour harmony had to be well planned. Six to eight ladies-in-waiting are sometimes on the screen at the same time, and the audience must be able to pick out people, not only by their faces and words, but also by dress. I tried to make groups of colours that blended, just as the cameraman must be able to form composition for colour. Then, too, every girl must be in the same style so as not to get out of period. We managed to get variation in the colours or headdress. In scenes with the queen, if her dress were trimmed with gold, I tried to have the ladies-in-waiting in shades of gold, to make an ensemble. Of course, at no time could any of the ladies-in-waiting outshine the queen in dress. Her clothes, however, were more tailored than was usual for that day, because she was the domineering type and her clothes reflected that quality. On Miss Lindfors' costumes I used tailored collars . . . had a lovely one designed, but it was uncomfortable and I created another. I also had to watch to make sure that the queen wasn't wearing the same collar as the Prime Minister or the King wore.

In contrast, the ladies-in-waiting were the light "giggly" type. For the most part I used dark colours for the queen because I felt they express royalty better—with light colours for accent. I saved the pastel shades for the ladies of the court and for the loves of Don Juan.

I worked with Travilla, the young designer with Tahitian background, in the designing of Errol Flynn's clothes, so as to make sure the colours blended.

Wardrobe plays a vital part in the glamorising of screen actresses. Barbara Bates and Helen Westcott realize this and watch attentively while Leah Rhodes discusses their costumes, which she has designed for " The Adventures of Don Juan."

I enjoy equally well dressing modern or historical females. But my first love is period costuming because doing Ingrid Bergman in period clothes for " Saratoga Trunk " was my first opportunity to be " on my own." I had been an assistant to Orry Kelly, an Australian, who, to my mind, is one of the greatest designers. He was head designer at Warner Bros. for more than ten years. Just when we faced the great problem of making of statuesque Ingrid Bergman a vivacious French girl, World War II started and Orry Kelly up and left for the army—leaving me with the problem. I was asked to do " Saratoga Trunk." I hardly thought they would start me with such an important assignment. I had had no ambition to be a designer on my own—I was afraid of the responsibility and I had had no real schooling as a designer. I had started out working in the Ladies' Wardrobe Department of Warner Bros. as a shopper, graduated into sewing, and later I was entrusted with a pair of scissors and permitted to cut the clothes which I, as a real woman, learned to love and appreciate. Orry Kelly had chosen me to help him sketch designs ; and, in spite of my lack of training, he told me that I had a natural flair. I improved with experience and before long I found myself adding and subtracting details of his excellent creations at his suggestion.

I was born in Port Arthur, Texas, of a middle-class family. My father loved drawing and I apparently inherited any talent I have from him. He was an orphan, born in New York, who went to Port Arthur when the town was starting in the oil business. He went to work for Gulf Refining Company when it had two small stills—it's now one of the largest in the world. He never had a chance to develop his talent for drawing—it was always there, though; for that reason he wasn't a business man. He encouraged it in me, however. It came out in two brothers—one is an architect, the other a commercial artist and portrait painter in Chicago; one sister studied interior decorating and loves to practise it in her own home. I love to do exterior decorating. I had only a very little training in high school, my sketching comes from practice, really. I do stylized sketches—I do not know anatomy too well, and do not try to draw fingers, toes, and so on. This way I get across the idea. I feel that stylized figures encourage design more. In my opinion, a designer should never emphasize faces or limbs, but should put all his effort into the dress that is being depicted. Just as a good photographer should concede defeat in the purpose of taking a picture if the background is noticed rather than the subject, as a designer I feel that by attracting too much attention to detail other than the dress I would defeat my purpose. I am laughed at for doing one-legged figures, but the design is the most important thing. Frequently I sketch my modern figures with my own hair-do—not that I consider it especially beautiful, but it's practical; consequently it goes into any design of particularly modern clothes.

I have reached my goal by doing what I do, but am always striving to do better. In this business there is always a new problem—you have never solved every one. In designing clothes I learn from my people the colours that they like and feel comfortable in, and stress their use. Women should be careful in their choice of colours—some react so strongly to their influence that many actresses have felt their performances to be affected.

One of the new necklines that will undoubtedly be soon inspired by " Don Juan " fashions is the " barrel " neckline; also the ruffed cuff and eave sleeves, which resemble the overhanging eaves on a house, thus achieving the width that is the substitute for shoulder pads which are now considered *passé*.

One of the most important phases of costume design is attention to accessories. For instance, in "Don Juan" gloves were designed especially for each and every costume; as much painstaking care was put into the embroidered details as into the costumes themselves.

Ingrid Bergman is wonderful to dress. For the first four changes in " Saratoga Trunk " she asked many questions and offered suggestions—after that I would just show her a sketch and she would say, " Oh, it's lovely." She got to the point where she didn't want to come up and fit—" They're always just right," she said. I had got the feeling of what she wanted.

I've had the pleasure of dressing three Scandinavian stars: Osa Massen, Ingrid Bergman and Viveca Lindfors. I seem to have had great luck with foreign stars—Hedy Lamarr and Lilli Palmer, whom I dressed for " Cloak and Dagger " and " My Girl Tisa." I'm looking forward to doing Lilli in modern clothes—so far, each time I've done her, she has been a poor girl and I'd like the chance to dress her up . . . she's the tiniest star I've had. Eleanor Parker, Eve Arden and Lauren Bacall are among the other stars I've dressed.

Designing clothes for stars is lots of fun and dressing a queen is tops for me, because I'd like every woman to look like a queen.

CLARK GABLE likes
to roam...with the  DESTINATION UNKNOWN

BECAUSE I'm a born wanderer—like to go fishing, like to hunt a bit—I've earned the reputation for being a modern Ike Walton and Daniel Boone rolled into one —a reputation that's sometimes embarrassing. I'm no expert, either on field or stream. I use simple tackle and shoot with an old Winchester minus any fancy gadgets. Avid fishermen and ardent hunters really make a business of it. And they talk a jargon of their own that leaves me well on the outside. For me, hunting and fishing are a good excuse to put on some old clothes, jump in the car, step on the gas and start exploring—destination unknown.

Of course, I have my favourite spots. Sometimes it's the Rogue River up in Oregon, or maybe the Big Hole Country in Wyoming (Wally Beery told me about that fisherman's paradise), or down across the Mexican border. Wherever I go I meet people—and people interest me a lot.

Sometimes, though, when I feel a spell of solitude coming on, I go fishing. I've often wondered how many men go fishing for the fish. I wonder if a lot of the time it's not just for the joy of sitting alone in a boat out in the centre of a lake, or standing in the middle of a stream where you've got nothing to worry about except the line, the fish and your thoughts. I read somewhere recently that two million Britons are interested in fishing : if they all were in dead earnest to get that fish on the line, well, it would be a bad day for our finned friends !

Herbert Hoover once remarked, " Fishing reduces our egotism, soothes our troubles and shames our wickedness. And," continued Mr. Hoover, " it is discipline in the equality of men—for all men are equal before fish ! " I think that's how it went, but it struck me Mr. Hoover had something.

In the American West there are really some wonderful places to hunt, to fish, to swap yarns and to see. You don't have to go very far from Hollywood—at least not by the seven-league-boot standards the vastness of the West has born into us. First the drive up the California coast is unforgettable. Oh yes, there's a super six-lane highway, but I'm not talking about that. Give me those little by-roads that take you off to quaint old towns the hurried world has all but forgotten. Two miles off the California Coast Highway there's a place called Solvang—a Danish settlement. No one ever heard of it until Rosalind Russell went up there to marry Carl Brisson. The momentary Hollywood visitation gave the natives something to talk about ever since.

Farther up the coast there's Pismo Beach—famous for clams, rum-runners (during American prohibition days) and surf fishing. Hollywood has invaded Pismo several times, notably for the beach scenes which Deborah Kerr and I did for "The Hucksters." But Pismo, like Solvang, soon returns to its quiet week-days and boisterous Saturday nights. Then there's Avila, the Portuguese fishing village, and pine-studded Cambria where Swiss Italians dominate the scene.

Sometimes the roads to these just-off-the-track places are of the washboard variety, or cut right out of the mountains like a narrow, twisting shelf—the mountains on one side and the sea, a few hundred feet below, on the other. No, not exactly the roads for a nervous driver, but I'm used to any old road.

M.G.M.'s famous star, Clark Gable, has a quiet smoke in the peace of his lovely garden.

Doubtless you've read about or seen the Monterey Bay country. Monterey and Carmel are not exactly off-the-track by any means, but often pleasure-seekers who throng the golf courses, the Pebble Beach Lodge and the 17-Mile Drive (comparable to Amalfi or the Grand Corniche) miss the old adobe Customs House where the flags of three nations—Spain, Mexico and the Stars and Stripes—have taken their turn when Monterey was California's capital. In Monterey, too, yet stands the first theatre in California and the house where Robert Louis Stevenson wooed Fanny Osborne.

I wouldn't have known these things except one day, while driving along "Cannery Row," the locale of Steinbeck's famous novel, I saw a sign that said: "Follow the red line to see the historic points of interest in Monterey." I looked, and there, down the centre of the street, sure enough, was a red line. Obediently I followed it as it turned corners and led me from one fascinating old building to another, on a sort of "serve yourself" Cook's Tour.

Most of the fishing up here is of the commercial variety (sardines) but I have cajoled good-natured Portuguese and Italian trawler captains to take me along. Between the smell of the fish and the fuel oil and the ground swells—well, it's fun, but landlubbers, beware!

After you leave Monterey there's a drive that never tires me—through the Santa Cruz Mountains where the giant redwood trees tower to heights of two and three hundred feet, are often more than one hundred feet in circumference and one, the General Sherman Tree, is 5,000 years old! Grizzly bears used to roam these hills but all the hunting is of a more modest variety now.

Clark Gable likes to jump in his car and go wandering up the Californian coast—destination unknown.

I'd like to tell you about my hideouts in San Francisco, too, but those are a story in themselves. Crossing the Golden Gate Bridge you hit Marin County—another empire of redwoods. One really rugged road leads to Drake's Bay and rewards you with quail and history. The quail are probably descended from birds that saw Sir Francis Drake land here to career the " Golden Hind " and claim Nova Albion (as he called California) for Good Queen Bess. The Queen had other fish to fry, or quail to hunt, however, and was more concerned with the Armada and Spanish galleons than Nova Albion. So, California became a part of New Spain rather than " Nova Albion."

Don't think I learned this from the history books—I didn't. I'd stopped at a country store and was yarning with an old-timer. I think my mentioning the quail brought it up. It seems that back in 1933 another fellow was hunting quail in the same spot. His chauffeur got restless waiting for his boss, got out of the car, and started pacing up and down the muddy road. He hit something sharp with his foot, dug around a while, and picked up the object. It was an old piece of metal, about eighteen inches square, and had some strange writing on it. The chauffeur said it looked like Chinese.

Anyway, he put it in the pocket of the automobile, thinking it might be handy for something—maybe to fix the car. It stayed there for several weeks until one day, many miles from where he found the metal plate, he cut himself on its sharp edge and threw it out into a field, probably uttering a few firm expletives as he did it. A few years later a ribbon clerk in an Oakland department store went on a picnic. He sat down under a tree and also cut himself on a sharp piece of metal—this same plate that the chauffeur had hurled from the car. The young guy probably said some nasty things about the metal plate, too,

Lana Turner and Clark Gable, teamed as screen sweethearts for the third time in M.G.M.'s " Homecoming." They portray the roles of an Army doctor and nurse who meet and fall in love while serving overseas. Here the cameraman has caught them off guard having a friendly chat between scenes. Gable and Miss Turner have appeared together previously in " Honky Tonk " and " Somewhere I'll Find You."

but as he sat there picnicking he studied the strange characters on its surface. Down in one corner he could just faintly see the letters D-R-A-K. Yes, you guessed it : The plate was tested by scientists and studied by historians and proved to be the brass marker that the intrepid Sir Francis (except he hadn't been knighted then) had placed with the British flag on the soil of California. The ribbon clerk got a reward of several thousand dollars and it is said that the chauffeur is still muttering about that blankety-blank plate !

The old timer told me the famous brass marker is on exhibit at the University of California in Berkeley, across the bay from San Francisco. I have not had a chance to see it yet, but I'm going. You see why I'm interested in people ? You learn something every time.

A few miles on from Drake's Bay another phase of Old California is rediscovered : Bodega Bay, Ross and Sebastopol—names reminiscent of the days when Russia cast a longing eye on California. The Russians were hunters, too, and traded with the Indians for furs. They built a fort and established a trading post but the Spaniards didn't like the idea so finally the Russians cleared out, sold their fort, trading post and lands to a genial Swiss gentleman named Johann Sutter. It was at one of Captain Sutter's sawmills, over in another part of the State, that gold was discovered exactly one hundred years ago this year—the gold that started the famous Rush and put California on the map.

My favourite fishing standby is the Rogue River in Oregon, not far over the California line. This is the one place I get fancy with the fishing gear and pull out my spinner and crawfish tail baits. If I get very fancy I invest in some flies. The Rogue is famous for steelhead, the king of all trout. The steelhead is a fighter and the average size is from five to ten pounds. If you want a real thrill, try fighting a five or ten pounder with light trout tackle ! It's an experience ! I know it sounds easy but if you haven't met a steelhead you don't know how game, savage and quick a fish can be.

But don't get me on steelhead or the Rogue River Country or I might use up all the rest of the pages in the book.

Yes, I like to hunt, fish, explore, meet old-timers and tenderfoots. Whether it's the California coast, the desert, the mountains, quail or steelhead— it suits me best when it's " Destination : Unknown."

When Clark Gable isn't wandering, he enjoys his 22-acre ranch in the San Fernando Valley. Keen on many forms of sport, he is shown here with one of his favourite hunting dogs.

MUSIC is the mother of FANTASY

by Walt Disney

MAN learned to sing before he could talk.

And he's still inclined to express himself most satisfactorily when his words are set to music or when his simple melodies are self-evident—when he wants to romance, to clown, to pour out his troubles or to celebrate his triumphs.

Music is indeed the mother of fantasy, of man's dreams and longings.

We who deal in fantasy as entertainment must therefore have a great and special respect and care for music as a complement to the animated screen cartoon.

Moviegoers will have observed that all our feature films have emphasized music, most of it especially written for our pictures, from the first full-length cartoon, " Snow White and The Seven Dwarfs," to our latest production, the forthcoming " Melody Time."

The measure of our success in meshing the visual and the musical elements in the Disney product, I believe, is in the care with which we create, find, or adapt our songs and our melodic score.

This is a vastly more important consideration than it is with the standard live-action screen drama, even when the latter are filmusicals. In our case, the songs, in addition to their lyrics, must maintain the oft-times delicately balanced mood of fantasy built up by the cartoon animations. Songs must not snap the spell, either when the animated characters themselves seem to chant the lyric, or when the songs are sung off-stage by such show-world celebrities as Nelson Eddy, Dinah Shore, Dennis Day, Roy Rogers, the Andrews Sisters, Sons of the Pioneers, or even in person, as companion to the cartoon characters, as James Baskett does in " Song of the South."

Song and scene, music and character, mood and performance, all must be particularly of a piece in screen fantasy, either when it is all cartoon or a combination of living actors and cartoon personages.

That is why so much of our music is written directly for the picture. And why, too, I am happy to say, it has the quality to appeal to the popular fancy and reach the best-seller lists.

From my earliest movie efforts, I realized that the kind of fantasy I intended to produce would require music in a special and often a lavish way. And also that I would have to approach it through unconventional channels. It would have to be a definite part of my medium. It would have to help very materially to tell a story, to round out visible characterization—have to be unique in character as well as presentation.

My first efforts to wed the moving picture and the vocal novelty were the " Silly Symphonies." I learned a lot from them—much of it so fundamental to the Disney type of production that it has been retained to this day : matters of audience appeal.

Our most pretentious undertaking with respect to music was " Fantasia." In that production we reversed the usual procedure

In " Make Mine Music," Nelson Eddy used his fine voice to sing three different roles—as tenor, as baritone, as bass. He enacted the part of Willie the Whale, whose ambition was to sing in Grand Opera.

of adapting the music to the scene, by creating animation effects to fit great classical music and so got stupendous spectacle, awesome scenes, delicate fantasy, burlesque parody and idyllic beauty, as was generally acknowledged.

Two other basically musical productions have been made at our Burbank studios, " Make Mine Music " and " Melody Time," the latter slated for release this autumn. Both rely on tune as much as text to present the assorted sequences in a single mood or comedy and playful romance. In the case of " Make Mine Music," audience response has amply sustained our venture in the musical cartoon format. " Melody Time " follows the approved pattern again, as an interlude between other feature-length fantasies of the kind represented by " Snow White," " Pinocchio," " Dumbo," " Saludos Amigos," " Bambi," " Song of the South," and the forthcoming " Alice in Wonderland," " The Little People " of Irish legend, " Peter Pan," and a saga of American legend.

In all these, music has had and will have a prominent part.

And because of our " philosophy " of musical application to screen fantasy and our method of presentation, each of our features has had its memorable songs. " Snow White " had its marching work-song chanted by the Seven Dwarfs ; " Bambi " still and again echoes its forest rhapsody, " Gay Little Spring Song " ; " Saludos Amigos " introduced the stirring " Samba " to coincide with a wave of dance rhythm from Latin America ; " Song of the South " brought the buoyant " Zip-a-Dee-Doo-Dah " from the lips of James Baskett as Uncle Remus—a hit parade item for months ; " Fantasia " had Stravinsky's awesome " Rite of Spring " and Moussorgsky's macabre " Night on Bald Mountain " ; " Make Mine Music " featured an entire miniature opera, with Nelson Eddy in the guise of the " Whale Who Wanted to Sing at the Met." ; in " Fun and Fancy Free " Dinah Shore chants the raffish revel of the woods, " A Bear Always Says It With a Slap " ; and " Melody Time " will keynote " Pecos Bill," a western regional, " Blue Shadows on the Trail," sung by Roy Rogers, and a solemn hymn, in contrast, sung by Dennis Day in the character of Johnny Appleseed, " The Lord Is Good to Me."

The voice of fantasy !

It is no haphazard song writer's impulse which makes him so often use the word " dreaming " in his melodic effusions. Song incorporates casual and superficial " dreaming " but also great vistas and desires of the spirit which spends so much of a lifetime in the realm of fantasy. This is obvious, of course, on a moment's reflection. We've made a sort of creed of it in our pictures : fit the song to the scene so that the two are one.

Preparation of our songs and scores is given much time and thought, from the very inception of a picture. Often a musical theme may indeed inspire the course of the story action and the very character of the cartoon actors. Nothing is more important in the early stages of the production, when the story is still flexible, than our musical conferences at the studio. Composers and arrangers and our story men and animators sit down together and work co-operatively on the problems involved and the ends desired. Themes are discussed, characters appraised, relationship between the animation actors worked out, tempo of scene and mood of story set, and complex technical requirements for a cartoon filmusical considered in every detail.

Music always has been a part of my thinking and planning and approach to picture-making from my earliest screen efforts. I worked out musical novelties and surprises even before the advent of sound on film.

An early effort was synchronized action, in 1922, between an organist who played an accompaniment to " Stumbling " on the screen. A spotlight was on the organist, and what transpired on the screen was presumably his dream as he stumbled around the world.

In 1924-25 I put an agile animated cat on the screen which in pantomime actually directed a full orchestra in the theatre pit, and which " spoke " with the voice of a man behind the screen.

These and other similar musical adjuncts to cartoon action in the early days of our medium naturally were based largely on the very newness and strangeness of photographs and photographed drawings in motion. They merged gradually into the more complicated and more integrated processes of animation as our medium expanded and its novelties were fully accepted as one of the major phases of screen entertainment.

Fantasy in our manner and our subject matter is now unthinkable without its complement of music—not mere sound and melodic clowning, but fine music, representative music, to touch the heart and beguile the mind of the moviegoer who is at all responsive to imaginative adventure.

Someone outside the picture is making the dickens of a noise. Could it be Jerry Colonna ? Anyway, Andy Russell, Walt Disney and Dinah Shore don't want to hear him.

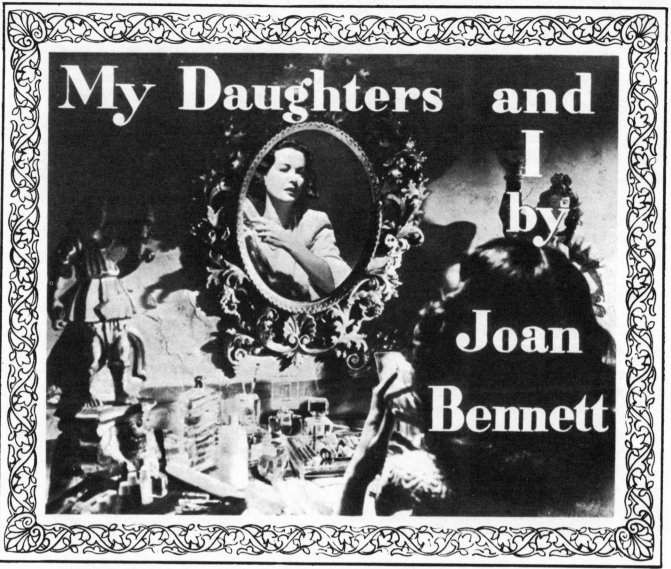

My Daughters and I

by Joan Bennett

THE problem of raising daughters in Hollywood usually centres itself around the lessons parents teach their children, and the methods which are employed in the completion of this instruction. And, as you read of these various methods of education, too often you get the feeling that parents give all and gain little.

I, for one, disagree. In their own way, children are just as effective teachers for their parents. While the young receive, they give much, and the learning process for mothers and fathers can be just as effective as the lessons they teach their offspring.

Actually, I've been taught a good deal by my three daughters. My girls are in varying age groups, and instead of being limited to one bracket, I gain varying bits of information from three distinct viewpoints. Diana is 19, and she has the sub-deb attitude. Melinda is 13 and very romantic at the moment, and from my 4-year-old Stephanie I get a baby's curious and frank observations.

First of all, I'll say that time never lags when my young ladies are around me. Naturally, they have different outlooks on the world around them, and to keep up with them, I'm mentally stimulated by this challenge.

My girls have helped me to relive my younger years, and from them I understand why I did so many things as a girl which I never fully understood. Now, when I see

Diana facing the same dilemma which once seemed so tremendous to me, I not only understand my early confusion, but I'm able to offer her some assistance.

While we're on this subject of assistance, I'd like to say that it has been my policy never to insist or demand that my family must follow a certain pattern. If Diana or Melinda decide they'll wear a certain costume with which I disagree to a party, rather than forbid it, I reason with them about their choices. It's surprising how successful this method usually is, and it brings a closer bond between us.

My daughters have developed in me a sort of selflessness that has grown out of my deep-seated interest in their own problems. I'm so busy trying to understand them that I have little time for any worries of my own.

I think I've acquired a tolerance of the problems of the young, and I've learned how tremendously important these problems can be to those in their formative years. I watch them trying to make decisions, and as they sift their various pros and cons, they help me distinguish the trivial from the serious.

Have you ever noticed how an interest in someone else's concern always makes your own seem less important? Things which I once thought were mountainous have lessened with the years. I believe that a sharing of any problem halves its seriousness.

Too many parents tend to scoff at their daughters' romance and dating problems, but they can learn a good deal in this. To a young girl, her boy-friends and their feelings for her are of vital importance, and she dresses up her sentiments with an amazing " flossiness."

It may seem inane to adults, but underneath it all there is a sincerity, and an almost idyllically romantic aura which she has built around herself as the central figure. She draws from pure fiction, and she quite happily makes a great thing of it.

Here is where most parents can observe and be reminded that perhaps they themselves are not making enough of their own affections for each other. Too often married people settle down into a commonplace, uneventful groove, and their love becomes an accepted and unexciting thing.

Joan Bennett, one of Hollywood's loveliest mothers, finds that keeping up with her daughters Stephanie (aged 4½), Diana (aged 19), and Melinda (aged 13), helps to keep her youthful in outlook.

In " Secret Beyond the Door," Joan Bennett had British actor Michael Redgrave as her leading man. Here she is relaxing off the set in a new type of reclining chair.

Romance must be kept youthful and vibrant with imagination, and where can you find more of this than in the mind of the teen-age girl who's experiencing the first pangs of love ? It should warm the heart of any parent to see anything as significant as this to a young, impressionable girl.

My daughters have given me a new understanding of the benefits of religion. As a girl, I studied certain phases of theology, but as a rule I missed the full import of the meaning because of my youth and inexperience in mystic comprehension.

When each girl started to Sunday School, naturally I accompanied her, and each Sunday I began to look forward more and more to this. Little by little I found myself getting a re-education and re-awakening to religion and its full meaning.

To me now, a Sunday when I haven't gone to church seems incomplete. Church attendance has given me a new philosophy of life which I find most helpful : that parents should require their children to do as they do, rather than do as they say. Through this they find for themselves a very wholesome mode of life.

Best of all, strict following of the rules of the Church has given me a tremendously satisfying feeling, because I've learned to realize that this observance is honesty in its highest form.

Last year, when Diana graduated from her finishing school, I attended the exercises and dressed as I thought the mother of a 19-year-old girl should. I wore a rather matronly outfit, and tried to look older, but when Diana caught one glimpse of me, she exploded.

After she caught her breath, she chided me for not dressing as I would usually dress. In trying to put on a few years, I had missed the effect completely !

Before Diana married, she studied art, and worked in a large department store and as a part-time model. When it comes to clothes preferences, I find that I'm most alert to her selections, because she's aware of even the most minute changes in the fashions.

Children keep their parents stimulated mentally, and keep them alive to this fast-moving world and all the daily events which fill the news columns. Once upon a time I used to skim briefly through the newspapers, but I now check them carefully, because we have frequent breakfast-table conversations on the important happenings of the day.

Melinda is particularly anxious to have our opinions, as she is extremely interested in a contemporary history course she is taking at her school. So, her requests for information put us on our mettle, and in order to speak intelligently on a given subject, it is necessary for us to follow closely the events of the day.

Actually, parents go through a constant refresher course with their children. The other day Melinda wanted some help with her algebra, and I tried to give it. After a half-dozen tries, I realized that my former mathematical skill had diminished considerably, and finally I had to call in the maid. Since that time, I've gone back to the textbook and brushed up, and I find that algebra is a lot more fun than I ever remembered it to be. Furthermore, I get a big kick out of checking Melinda's finished problems.

I've learned to swim, for instance, because I felt " left out of things " when the girls have been having fun around the pool, and very shortly I discovered that as my physical stamina increased, I derived more enjoyment with my added energy out of the 24 hours of each day.

My girls have given me a deeper appreciation of good music, both in the classical and modern field, and I find now that I'm a more attentive audience because I listen both with their ears and mine. And, in addition, seeing so many things through my daughters' eyes as well as my own, I've led a doubly full life.

25 changes of wardrobe were necessary for Joan Bennett in her latest picture "Secret Beyond the Door." Here she is studying Travis Banton's sketches.

GET THAT PROP...

by 'LIMEY' PLEWS MASTER OF PROPERTIES · WARNER BROS.

UNLESS one is close to the business, the property man is an unknown quantity. Film audiences seldom give him a thought. Why? Because it's his business to see that everything goes smoothly, that the director gets everything he asks for on a set, that every little thing " matches up "—and it does. Without the property man who knows his business, a picture would be just a plain mess.

I have been given some tough jobs in my day. For instance, the very first prop I was asked to get when I started in film business was a Roman tear vase. I went to the research department and looked at a picture of it. It was a little vase worn on a necklace. Off I went. To show you what good luck I had, it so happened I had to get some rings for Bette Davis, and for those I had to go to a particular jeweller—a Mr. Crouch. It was unbelievable but when I showed him the sketch of the tear vial—never dreaming he had one —he said, " I have exactly what you are looking for." It was. My luck was just too good.

How I happened to come to Hollywood? I met Roland B. Lee, a Yankee officer, who was in a hospital in France with me, right after the Battle of Amiens. He told me, " Limey, I am a Hollywood director. If you ever come to Hollywood, I can do things for you. Look me up." I didn't think too much of that promise at that time and I don't think Lee meant too much when he said that. But as things have a way of going, my family, after the war was over, moved to Canada and there I remembered Lee. Young as I was, I decided to risk a long shot. I didn't leave my family in peace until I had convinced them that Hollywood was the place for us. We left Winnipeg to try our luck in Hollywood.

First thing that worried me when coming to Hollywood was how to look up Mr. Lee. I found out he was working at the Fox Studio. I went there, not knowing about the studio gatemen. I was turned away. But then I also noticed that a bunch of fellows in British uniforms passed uninhibited through the gates. Somebody tipped me off that they were movie extras. So, like a flash, I had an idea. I went straight home, put on my uniform which still fitted me because I had never gained an ounce of weight, and walked right past the gateman. Lee was as good as his word. Things were easier in the studios then than now and I was put to work right then and there as an assistant property man. He liked me, I liked the work, and the family liked Hollywood—and everything was likes. And what's more, I still like it. I am now first property man but if you give me my full title, I am a Warner Brothers master of properties.

For most of my problems and headaches, Michael Curtiz is responsible. What now is known at the Warner lot as a " Mike Curtiz' Nightmare Prop " came up when we were making " Bright Lights," with Dorothy Mackaill. Mike comes to me and says, " Limey, you give me cake with a design on it that shows Honolulu, with boys riding surf boards, palm trees and stuff." I took my problem to Charlie, the chef, and I said, " Charlie,

I'm giving you this order way ahead. I need it in three weeks." One day, without my knowing it, Michael saw Charlie in the studio canteen. "You're making a cake for me, Charlie?" asked Michael. "Ya," says the chef. He is Swiss. "Charlie, the cake must be so-oo big," Curtiz said with his Hungarian accent and scrambled English, stretching his arms out and telling the chef what he wanted. About a week later I went to the canteen to have my lunch and I noticed a crowd of people pulling down a wall to bring out an enormous cake. It must have been nine-feet in diameter and about twelve-feet high, with four layers. "Publicity," I figured, "Boy! they're great." I sit down and order my lunch, and when the waitress brought me my dessert, I was reminded of the cake. It was as if something choked me. I dropped my fork and dashed to the cake. And I felt all heaven breaking down over me. Sure enough it had the Honolulu design. I ran to Charlie. "I can't use that cake," I screamed. "Mr. Curtiz ordered this," he said. I ran to Mike, "If Hal Wallis (he was the producer on the picture) sees that, he will tear us apart and throw us out," I yelled. Mike ran with me back to the canteen where about thirty men were trying to lift the cake through the hole in the

" Limey " Plews has the difficult job at Warner Bros. of *" Getting that Prop."* No matter what the obstacles, *" Limey "* has always succeeded in getting what was needed.

wall. Well, Michael did some fast thinking and I did too, and I came up with an idea. " Mike," I says, " if we don't want to get fired, we have got to use the cake. The leading lady, at the party, must go up on the ladder and cut the cake. You'll have to find a way to shoot that scene." I think Michael is the smartest director in Hollywood and I found that out just then, because he gave orders to get a camera boom, one of those huge cranes, and actually we shot the scene with the boom. And that was the first time a camera boom was used in sound pictures. I claim this to be my contribution to motion picture history. I had to get a few cakes since then for Michael. We needed one for Cary Grant's birthday party in " Night and Day," and the last one I had to get was for Michael Curtiz' own picture, " The Unsuspected," wherein Claude Rains has a birthday party. Mike lets me do the ordering. He has learned his lesson and found out that he can't have his cake and order it too.

To give you some idea of what a property man has to go through, I'll give an illustration. We were making a picture many years ago for Warner's, right in the heart of the desert. In our prop cars we always carry artificial flowers because you never know when you may need some. But Michael Curtiz got an idea that he wanted the leading man to give his leading lady real honest-to-God flowers. He made me go out with my crew 110 miles to a train stop. We bribed the engineer and the stewards with smokes, for smokes are always good currency, and we robbed the dining car of all the flowers they had. When we came back, Curtiz looked at the flowers, then at me and, completely unaware of the difficulties we had in getting them, said, " Why didn't you get me orchids ? "

SPECTACULAR BOSS

by Faith Domergue

HOLLYWOOD'S young hopefuls refer to Howard Hughes as the Miracle Man of the industry, with a silent prayer that the dynamic aviator-producer may see fit to divert some of his star-making magic to their own careers.

I am one of the lucky few to whom the miracle has happened. I only hope that my performance in " Vendetta " will justify Howard's faith in Faith and, at the same time, prove me a worthy successor to all the previous Hughes discoveries, a glittering galaxy of stars, including the late beloved Jean Harlow, Ann Dvorak, Paul Muni, Pat O'Brien, George Raft and my good friend Jane Russell.

It is Howard's established custom not to engage stars but to create them. Jean Harlow was an unknown before " Hell's Angels " catapulted her to the topmost rung of the ladder of fame. In " Scarface," forerunner and most successful of the gangster cycle, Howard played a triple parlay and in one thrust established Paul Muni, George Raft and Ann Dvorak as ranking screen personalities. The Hughes magic, applied to Jane Russell, fashioned one of the most popular favourites of recent years. Jane's success continues to skyrocket since "The Outlaw," and Jane herself would be the first to give the lion's share of the credit to her spectacular boss.

When I met him some five years ago, over lunch on his yacht at Balboa, one of our loveliest Pacific coast resorts, I little dreamed of the rigorous training that lay ahead of me before I would become a star. When he offered me a long-term contract I was first stunned, then intoxicated, by visions of my name dancing in lights on the nation's marquees. But those glamorous visions faded and the lights dimmed

Faith Domergue is director Howard Hughes' latest discovery. She stars in a Corsican melodrama " Vendetta." Right: fatally wounded by an assassin's bullet, she is dying in the arms of her brother, played by George Dolenz.

during the three years that followed, three long years in which I underwent a thorough overhauling at the hands of an army of expert tutors and coaches, physical instructors, hair stylists, costumers and make-up technicians. Howard is a perfectionist and no factor was to be overlooked in my bid for stardom.

What had interested Hollywood's most eligible unmarried producer in the first place was my Latin appearance. I am a Creole, of pure French and Spanish descent. My education in the French schools of New Orleans and in Spanish convents on the Pacific coast had doubtless accentuated my European background. So it was only natural, I suppose, that when Howard Hughes was looking for an actress to portray the part of Colomba in his Corsican melodrama, " Vendetta," he should have given me a second look.

A lightning sketch of Howard's multi-faceted personality would reveal that, on being orphaned at eighteen, he took over the management of his parents' manu-facturing concern and that he forthwith ran a $300,000 inheritance into a fortune estimated today at $125,000,000. One might expect that, having written his own personal entries into the history of aviation and the motion picture industry, the enigmatic Texan would be content to rest on his laurels and enjoy the benefits of his mammoth fortune. Yet Howard welcomes new responsibilities with every new expansion of his business interests and he regularly works around the clock, often seven days a week.

He has been decorated by his government and has won every major aviation award. He has also won the Motion Picture Academy Award. Three-

" *Spectacular Boss* " *Howard Hughes, having fashioned such stars as Paul Muni and the late Jean Harlow, has introduced Jane Russell (left) and Faith Domergue to the film-going public.*

fourths of the drills used in the world's oil industry come from the Hughes Tool Company. Many of the world's most outstanding air speed records were chalked up by Howard, and his round-the-world flight mark stood for nearly a decade.

One could list the infinite variety of the Hughes interests and activities indefinitely. The first peace-time application of radar is another Hughes credit. He invented an ammunition feed which saved countless Allied airplanes and thousands of American lives during the last war. He was also the army's largest supplier of cannon. He owns and operates one of the largest breweries in the country and controls the vast interests of the Trans World Airlines. He also helped to design the Constellation airplane, the international standard modern air transport, as well as many other aircraft for commercial and military use.

While Howard's film activities started as a rich man's hobby, his Magic Touch quickly turned them into one of his major interests. He was barely twenty-one when, vacationing in California, he met an actor named Ralph Graves who had an idea for a movie but needed a backer. Howard backed Graves' film to the tune of $40,000, then shelved the finished product because he thought it was too bad to be released.

The gauntlet had been thrown at his feet, however, and he speedily turned out a second production, " Everybody's Acting," which had a sensational success. It was Howard's third picture, though, which placed him in the front row of the cinema moguls, a comedy called " Two Arabian Knights " which won the Motion Picture Academy's Award as the year's best comedy.

Followed successful productions under the Hughes name like " The Racket " and " The Mating Call," and then came the picture that was to make screen history, " Hell's Angels." Completed as a silent picture, it cost $3,000,000, an unheard of figure at that time. Howard had outspent Hollywood's biggest spenders to hire expert pilots, flying real airplanes in real air battles to give his picture the authenticity his sense of perfection demanded.

Then Howard saw his first talking picture and decided that he must remake " Hell's Angels." to keep pace with progress. The $4,000,000 finished version of " Hell's Angels," the most expensive production ever filmed at that time, assured the spectacular career of the late Jean Harlow and grossed more than $8,000,000.

After originating the cycle of huge aviation spectacles on the screen, Howard was determined to prove that these successes could be topped. In rapid succession he turned out " Scarface " and " The Front Page," first of the screen's outstanding newspaper dramas. Both of these pictures were among the top box-office successes of the early thirties.

" The Outlaw," perhaps the most widely publicized picture in history, introduced Jane Russell and has smashed box-office records wherever it has been shown throughout the United States, despite a storm of censorship difficulties in certain localities.

And now " Vendetta "! Once again Howard has shattered old concepts and replaced them with new precedents for the industry to adopt. That is why it is so stimulating to work for Howard. By playing in a Hughes' picture one is assured of the liveliest critical attention and, when one is fortunate enough to be rewarded with stardom, the end of the rainbow is in sight, as can be attested by the glittering careers of previous proteges on whom Howard has conferred the benefit of his Magic Touch.

INGRID BERGMAN HAD A DREAM

by VICTOR FLEMING

WE all dream, some very timidly, some very boldly, of one very particular thing that we should like to see realized. Most dreams are in vain, but a Swedish actress, Ingrid Bergman, had her dream come true—not once, but twice. The first time, when she stepped before an audience at the Alvin Theatre in New York as Joan of Lorraine; the second in the darkness of a projection room when she saw the first rushes of herself on the screen as Joan of Arc.

I have never discussed with Miss Bergman the origin of her desire to play Joan, but I do know it was an ambition she has had all her life. She gave up the opportunity of doing several important films and the very large salaries involved, so deep-rooted was the desire to play Joan on the stage.

I went to New York and saw the play. As I watched Ingrid Bergman walk out on that stage and take complete possession of it, I thought : How few actresses could do it ! She has a strength—the strength of her Viking ancestry, and a strange quality of physical and mental vitality, a simplicity tinged with the Continental touch. Yes, here was a Joan well worth bringing to the screen. I invited her to lunch. " Ingrid, you were magnificent ! You ought to play Joan for the rest of your life," I told her. Her eyes gleamed. " It's the fulfilment of a great dream," she said. " Let's finish the dream and bring Joan to the screen," I returned. " I will talk it over with Walter Wanger (he is the eminent producer). We will have Maxwell Anderson and Andrew Solt do the screenplay ; and you, Walter and I will form our own company. I will direct the film."

We finished our lunch and I began to make the plans that brought to the screen a simple account, honestly told, of one of the greatest women in history : Joan of Arc. And, in my opinion, gave a great actress the finest role of her career.

The bringing of Joan to the screen is a story in itself. The budget was set at $4,600,000.

At a council-of-war meeting with French army leaders, Joan of Arc (Ingrid Bergman) agrees that she will issue no direct orders to the soldiers—but she expects the generals to rally the men to her. The scene is from Sierra-R.K.O.'s forthcoming Technicolor production " Joan of Arc."

Ninety-five people were engaged to set up a skeleton staff of the technical departments. Three people took charge of research—the most important factor of all the preparatory work—and what a stupendous job they undertook. The events of Joan's life, each day, if possible, from January 1, 1429 to May 30, 1430, had to be established. The first discovery was a bombshell when it was found that it was not proper in the 15th Century to write about personal characteristics. There were no documents describing the personal appearance of Joan or any of the characters who stormed through her life. All had to be re-created, the modes, manners and personal appearances of all characters in the script, from Joan to the King of France, from Joan's father to the lowest pageboy in the court. There were seventy-seven principal roles in the picture. Then there was the matter of

The " First Lady of the Screen " had a dream—that she would one day play the role of Joan of Arc. That dream has been twice realized, for Ingrid Bergman enacted this great part both on the stage and in the forthcoming film " Joan of Arc." It is likely to be the greatest performance of her outstanding career.

armour. It took Leonard Heinrich, armourer of New York's Metropolitan Museum, 600 hours to fashion Joan's armour of aluminium. It was done by hand. It weighed twenty pounds, but, at that, Miss Bergman was luckier than the real Joan whose armour weighed sixty pounds.

A terrific problem was the 150 suits of armour that had to be made by mass production for the rest of the cast.

Noel Howard, our armour expert, stood in long woollen underwear while a prototype in a plaster cast was made. A speedboat builder stamped out the dyes. A ton and a third of magnesium was used. The manufacturing period covered three months.

The armour for the picture is Gothic; it is severe and practical with no unnecessary adornments.

We still chuckle at the efforts of the actors when they first tried to stand up in the armour. Some of them fell flat on their faces when they attempted to walk. By degrees everyone got used to the cumbersome stuff.

Ingrid Bergman has Charles Boyer for her lover and leading man in the filming of Eric Remarque's "Arch of Triumph."

Among other unusual things to be re-created were the candles that reached from floor to dome in the cathedral; the tiny ampoule of holy oil; the giant organ—they all had to be as if loaned by the medieval archbishop himself—all these for the coronation of King Charles VII in the Gothic cathedral at Rheims. Joan arrived for the ceremony which took place one fateful Sunday, July 17, 1429.

Michel Bernheim, one of the research team and a lifelong student of the Joan story, aided in the translation of the half dozen volumes written by Jules Quicherat about the two trials Joan was subjected to, one at Rouen where she was tried as a heretic, and the rehabilitation trial which took place twenty-five years after her martyrdom. This last trial cleared her name and re-affirmed her faith.

Miss Bergman spared herself no personal effort in becoming Joan. Although she is an excellent horsewoman, she learned to ride all over again—the medieval way. Warriors in Joan's time rode stiff-legged in the saddle. They never sat and posted. For eight weeks she practised stiff-legged riding. People stared at the broom handle she carried in the pocket of her stirrup. But she had to get the feel of carrying a banner—she thought in practising the broomstick would be less conspicuous.

As the story unfolded in the script, we found we were unfolding history. It wasn't like doing Shakespeare—it wasn't doing a play; it was just a matter of presenting the historical facts we had found with an artistry that would spell entertainment. I hope the audience will think we accomplished it.

Pageantry was not where we expected it and it was impossible to reproduce certain phases of it, so it had to be omitted. But there was an over-abundance of material that we could use by staying very close to Joan and following her life. There is no leading man in the picture—there is a leading spirit; that's what the picture has: an emotion. It is all focused around an emotional theme.

The peasant quality of Ingrid Bergman served her well in carrying on the truly strenuous part of Joan. With her fine, strong body, she fitted the part well physically.

Of all the dozens of conceptions we looked at of the martyred peasant girl, no two of them were alike. In some she looked as if she had been conceived from a reproduction of Billy the Kid, one of our toughest Western characters; in another she was a good presentation of a medieval saint; in another she looked every inch a soldier, with great physical strength and power to wield a blade. Most of the reproductions conveyed a feeling she was older than her nineteen years—that was her age when she was executed. There is one small drawing, like a child's effort, drawn on the margin of one of the scribe's writing at the trial. It was a girl with a banner, but the face was very crudely drawn.

I found my interest growing each day as we went along with the picture. I had started with the idea principally because I knew it was the great dream of a great actress. When she left for New York to create Joan in the stageplay, I knew then how much it would mean to her to be given the opportunity to play Joan in the broader realm of the film. But once we started I found it all intensely fascinating.

Audiences all over the world will have the chance to see how people lived, walked, ate, and rode horses in the days when a peasant girl was destined to change the fortunes of France. We have tried to give authenticity to every detail of life 500 years ago in Mediæval France, and a true picture of the farm girl who gave her life in making a reality of a vision.

Rough French soldiers prepare to follow the simple peasant girl, Joan of Arc, as she receives a blessing and signet ring before departure.

Thoughts from a Hilltop
by Lew Ayres

I WAS born on a hill in Minneapolis, in a house called " Ayre Castle." Houses in America are seldom named—they are mostly known by numbers which, on account of the length of many streets, go into high digits, but our family liked the old country custom of naming houses. All the houses I have lived in have been named after our old home. A name gives a house an individuality. I like that.

My house stands on the top of one of the highest hills in Hollywood. It has a wide view and at night the numerous lights of the city below make a beautiful pattern. I have never been happy living down on the flats—I did for one year, but I wasn't contented until I got my house built on the hill where I hope to live always. It is wonderful up there.

Because I have a somewhat philosophical mind and like to express my ideas, people who must have a reason for everything say, " Oh! living on a hill as you do must give you great inspiration." I have not found this true—and when you think of many people living off in mountain places, it must be admitted they often are backward, uncultured and far from poetic people. Their life is hard; they do not have educational advantages and are too busy wresting a livelihood out of their surroundings to pay much heed to the beauty of the place.

But living on a hilltop has some distinctly practical advantages. Friends can be entertained without disturbing the neighbours—if we want to sing, play records, argue at the top of our voices, we can make all the noise we want and no one worries about it— unless it is the coyotes, the owls, the foxes and squirrels who share the neighbourhood with me.

While I like people, a hilltop has the advantage of making them think twice before " just dropping in " and many will not face the narrow, winding road leading to the house. This means I have a lot of time to myself—which is never too much, for my hobbies

Giving another of the sincere performances that have marked the return of Lew Ayres to the screen since his war service, Lew plays opposite Jane Wyman in Warner Bros.' "Johnny Belinda."

keep me busy both by night and day. I like to paint and my sketches are crowding me out of the house.

Another hobby is my weather bureau. When I open the door of my house, boom! the weather is right in my face. The people below discuss the weather, but up high I live in it. The wind and I became friends—so did the sun and the stars at night—the next thing I know I was buying all sorts of meteorological instruments and had set up means of really knowing what makes the wind blow and the temperature often capricious.

Because of the inaccessibility of my home to casual droppers-in, I have plenty of time for reading. I am a voracious reader. On my bookshelves volumes of history, philosophy, biology nudge the latest novel and detective yarn—but I have my favourites. It is one of my greatest hopes to bring " Pericles and Aspasia " to the screen. What a story, and what a background! The great objection is the money needed to screen it—it would cost a fortune. Another story I would like to do is that of " Heloise and Abelard," but Pericles is my first love because it is about an era comparable to our own. People would find it amusing, satirical and very pointed. They would get the enlightening ideas of Euripides and Socrates, and some idea of the birth of democracy—plus a great love story. To me it is more exciting and important than anything I have run across.

I often think of my first days in Hollywood—I worked in a jazz band. I was in my teens, and I liked music. There were four or five of us in the group. We looked on it all as a wonderful lark but we made very good money. We worked all the Mexican border towns—it was in them I got my first look at life in the raw. The Mexicans I met were generally very poor ; the only pleasure they get is in the small cantinas. The prosperity of their towns depended on the motley crowd so frequently seen in border towns. Artists, gamblers, traders—people of all nationalities mingle. I had a chance to observe an entirely new strata of life as I twanged my guitar.

Back in Hollywood I was dancing in the Blossom Room, as it was called in those days, of the Roosevelt Hotel. A tap on my shoulder startled me a little. My partner looked astonished. " Young man, how would you like to make a movie test ? " I said, " Why not ? "—although becoming a film actor had not entered my head. I was perfectly happy with the band. However, I made the test and was given a contract with Pathe at $75 a week—not bad for those days. M.G.M. asked me to play in " The Kiss." I was more than mildly excited at the prospect of playing opposite Greta Garbo, a truly great actress. From then on my acting career progressed steadily and I built my hilltop home.

I am particularly interested in the fate of children—maybe because I have never had the privilege of having children of my own. I do feel that they have been plunged into the type of misery that children should never have to endure. Many in Europe are forced to live under most unhappy conditions—without parents, in homes inadequate for warmth and shelter; clothes hardly worthy of the name often cover undernourished bodies. It is all horrible to think about, but it is something that has to be faced and remedied. That's why I offered to help in every way I can to raise funds for their care.

I have a great admiration for the Quakers, who, through all the world's troubles, have been permitted to go everywhere in their effort to lessen people's misery—especially that of the children. The overall policy of the Quakers is good and they have a practical form of showing brotherly love. I am not a Quaker, but I do have great respect for the way they build their lives around a set of rules and bide by them to the extent of doing much good in the name of their religion.

I am very interested in religion—so much so that I made a record album of Biblical stories, hoping to interest the children as well as their elders in the lives of Biblical characters. The album is named " Tales of Ancient Heroes." We presented our stories in play form, the roles were played by good actors; the music was appropriate and I did the narration. In making the album my hope was that it would prove interesting to Bible lovers and create an interest in those not so familiar with the colourful episodes in the greatest of books.

A picture I made for Warner Bros. recently was " Johnny Belinda." In it I played the part of a doctor who was interested in the development of an unhappy deaf mute who suffered greatly at the hands of her father and the townspeople of the Nova Scotian fishing village where she was born. In the story, Belinda has a child, not legitimate, and it was this happening that gave the story its plot. In the end I marry Belinda. The part was easy for me and interesting, too, because it dealt with the problem of the underdog. That is a subject I seem compelled to study. Why, I don't know—perhaps I can blame it on my hilltop—because, as I said before, living on a hilltop gives one plenty of time for thought—especially in Hollywood, where people have so much to do that a fellow who chooses to live off the beaten path can dwell in peace.

Four of the screens finest stars are teamed in " Johnny Belinda." Left to right, they are Agnes Moorhead, Jane Wyman, Lew Ayres and Charles Bickford. Agnes Moorhead will long be remembered for her brilliant performance in " The Magnificent Ambersons."

UP IN THE AIR

by GENE RAYMOND

THERE are many reasons why Hollywood is one of the most air-minded communities in the world. Of course, that statement might seem funny when you consider that Hollywood itself doesn't have an airport, an aircraft plant, or any plans for one. However, its neighbouring communities bristle with airports, huge aviation factories, flying schools, and allied interests. What I really mean when I say " Hollywood " is all the thousands of people connected with the motion picture studios—the actors, producers, directors, the technical workers, and even the office staff and post boys.

Hollywood's interest in aviation is natural. First of all, Southern California is the centre of the aircraft industry with the huge aviation plants of Howard Hughes, Douglas, Lockheed, North American, Northrop and Consolidated-Vultee—plants that turned out thousands of almost every type of aircraft during the war. Second, is the weather. Yes, it gets pretty foggy at certain times of the year but generally speaking, flying weather in Southern California is always pretty good. Third, and maybe the most important of all the reasons for our air-mindedness, is the terrific distances. Our " nearby " holiday resorts are not so nearby—the famed desert resort of Palm Springs is about 120 miles, Santa Barbara is almost 100, Las Vegas and its roulette wheels is nearly 300, Carmel, Monterey and Yosemite are over 350, and popular Rogue River, famous for its fishing, is more than 750 miles away. Yet, these are all places we like to go to for week-end and short vacations.

There is a special reason, however, why those of us in the film industry are aviation minded. Picture making is always a rush proposition. Getting places fast is important. Business trips to New York take three days on the fastest streamlined trains but can be accomplished in less than ten hours by plane. So naturally, when producers go east to consult with bankers and distributors, or stars go to see the latest plays (a " must " for everyone who takes acting seriously), or studio location managers go in quest of certain kinds of scenery—they usually go by plane.

Then, of course, many of us flew in the war and there are a surprising number of old-timers in the film business who flew also in World War I.

My interest in aviation started in 1939, right after England declared war. It was then that I started to take flying lessons. It didn't take much foresight to see

Gene Raymond at home on leave during the war, when he was an Army Air Corps flyer. Out of uniform now, he keeps in training with a Reserve Officers' Squadron, of which he is second-in-command.

that we were going to be in it and that " it " was going to be largely a battle in the air.

My wife, Jeanette MacDonald, worried a bit but kept her feelings to herself because in her heart she agreed that it was the smart thing to do. At first she was not so air-minded as I, but now I think I've won her over.

Right after Pearl Harbour I volunteered for everything—Navy, Marines, and Army. Unlike the British system, each branch of our fighting forces has its own air-arm so it didn't matter which it was because I knew there was a chance to get in the air regardless of which branch took me.

Early in 1942 I was commissioned in the Army Air Corps. As I told you, I had taken flying lessons and received a licence, but those lessons were nothing to those I got in the Army. They finally taught me to be a bombardier, fly B-25s and B-17 Flying Fortresses, and also to be an intelligence officer. I think B-25s are my favourite military planes. A large part of my schooling and much of my war duty was in England where I was with the 8th Bomber Command.

The Air Corps and I were a bit busy when I was in England but someday soon I hope to go over again with nothing to do but see the country. Jeanette enjoyed her trip last year when she went over to sing at the Albert Hall and next time she insists we go together. She has lots of things to show me.

Although I was placed on inactive duty late in 1945, I am keeping up my military flying. The government spent a good $35,000 training me and I don't want to let this expensive schooling go to waste, at least not until the world is war-proof. I'm afraid it is far from that right now.

At present I am second-in-command of a Reserve Officers' Squadron. We fly missions and formations at least four hours a month and have ten single- and multi-motored aircraft and 150 officers. Uncle Sam, of course, gives us the planes and the facilities.

I also have a commercial licence and frequently charter a plane and fly myself to various places on both business and pleasure. Many Hollywood people own their own planes but so far I have resisted the temptation to buy one. They are still very expensive to acquire and the cost of maintenance is way out of line. It is far cheaper to charter a plane at $20.00 an hour than to own one unless, of course, you commute between Hollywood and some distant point as many film people do. Clarence Brown, the M-G-M director, commutes each day from the private flying field at his ranch near Calabasas to the Culver City Airport which is a short drive to the studio.

Army flying almost spoils you for civilian air jaunting. I remember the days during the war when I taxied up to an airport with a B-17 and said, "Fill 'er up!" In went 1,700

Two of Hollywood's keenest private flyers are Veronica Lake and husband André de Toth. Both have their flying licences, and have piloted the plane shown in the background, which Veronica presented to her husband.

gallons and all I had to do was sign a chit and Uncle Sam paid the bill. Nowadays on private trips I look at the gauge, do a little computing, and meekly say, " Put in ten."

Despite the costs, many stars do own private planes. Veronica Lake presented a Navion to her director-husband, André de Toth, and they both took flying lessons in their spare time and now have their licences. Ty Power is one of Hollywood's most globe-trotting aviators and he has a couple of planes. One was cracked up, however, when he was on location in Mexico for " Captain from Castile." He was not in the plane when it happened but had loaned it to a member of the camera crew. Dick Powell, who also owns his own and got his licence back in 1927, is president of the Flying Service, a correspondence school for aspiring aviators which gives them all the book training they need up to the time when they are ready to take off on their first flight. Mrs. Powell—June Allyson—is not so air-minded as her spouse, however. Barbara Stanwyck is another wife who prefers to stay on the ground despite the fact that Bob Taylor's plane is a twin-engine job—one for both of them !

Frances Langford and Jon Hall also have a flying school as well as the agency for Ercoupes, an all-metal, low-wing ship operated entirely by simple hand controls. Robert Young is one of the students Hall instructs personally.

Gene Autry flies his Beechcraft, or one of his other two planes, all over the United States both for pleasure and on business trips. Edgar Bergen is another " capitalist " with two planes, a Navy Cessna and a Beechcraft. He also owns an airport in Montebello.

Hollywood's aviation pioneers are Ken Maynard and Wallace Beery. Both of them like to hunt and, as good hunting is far from Hollywood, they were among the first to take advantage of the air age. Beery has been in the air for thirty years and has flown over almost every state in the Union.

Robert Cummings, who also started flying before the war, evidently figured as I did that it was cheaper to charter than to own a plane and sold his ship to Charles " Buddy " Rogers, who is now producing pictures with his wife, Mary Pickford.

Others who fly, though they don't all own their own planes, are Joan Fontaine, Victor Fleming, Brian Aherne, Henry King, Ann Sheridan, Jimmy Stewart, Hal Roach, Jr., Lee Cobb, Rod Cameron, Brian Donlevy, and Warner Bros.' dance director, Le Roy Prinz.

Prinz flew in the Escadrille Lafayette in World War I and his office is lined with pictures of his two loves—beautiful girls and beautiful planes.

Errol Flynn is taking lessons in helicopter flying. In fact, so many in the movie colony are learning to fly that it is hard to keep track of them.

Although I've had my share of action pictures, the only one that was in any way connected with aviation was a musical I made many years ago, " Flying Down to Rio " in which I " flew " with Dolores Del Rio, Fred Astaire, and Ginger Rogers. Ironically, that was before I became a pilot.

My most recent picture is " Assigned to Danger," which I have just finished for Eagle Lion. My leading lady is an up-and-coming miss by the name of Noreen Nash. In this film I play the part of an insurance investigator. Maybe in my next picture I'll get a chance to fly. I hope so.

But whether I fly in films or not, aviation will always be one of my greatest interests. I don't predict that a day will come when we will all be flying. As my friend Ty Power said, " Flying will never be safe so long as you have to drive to the airport ! "

Californian Gardens are lovely
says
Greer Garson

MOST Californian gardens do quite well, even to the marigolds. Colourful flowers make the hillside gleam, sweeping front lawns transform almost every residential street into a parkway and the many varieties of trees for which California is famous create startling contrasts.

My Mother and I had been in Hollywood a very short time when we discovered there was somewhere new to go each weekend. We made many short trips up and down the coast. It was through these early weekend adventures that we found a dear little house in Carmel on the Monterey Peninsula. It intrigued me as being a wonderful hideaway when I had a holiday from the studio. It is in a cypress grove where we can hear the ocean and walk to the beach in just a few minutes. And, of course, the garden is always ablaze with flowers.

Gardens have always fascinated me, but with busy days at the studio it is only once in a while that I find time to do a bit of digging and planting myself. When I get home from the studio, if it is not too dark, I take a walk around the warden with Gogo, our large white French poodle. Sometimes Rama, the Siamese cat, comes trotting along with us. When Mother and I first came to· Hollywood we lived in Beverley Hills and our house there did not have too large a garden. Later we moved to Bel Air where we have a large enough garden for a good walk.

Ready for work, Greer Garson dons denims and starts in on the garden of her Pebble Beach cottage which overlooks the Pacific on the gorgeous Monterey Peninsular. Greer is a keen gardener, and tells you all about the flowers which she cultivates.

The house I bought in Bel Air is built in front of a hill on which California holly, wild lilac and other native shrubbery thrive. In the spring there is a sprinkling of wild flowers including the famous California golden poppy. The house itself is rather old fashioned and is shaded by very large sycamore trees. They were growing there when Indians wandered along the little stream which flows through the grounds at the back of the swimming pool. Now tall, graceful Australian tree ferns grow along the terraced bank and lilies of all types edge the path beyond. They grow well in the filtered shade of the tall hedge behind them.

137

Along the driveway leading to the front door is a row of gardenias. On either side of the doorway are camellia trees almost six feet high. When the gardenias bloom the air is heavily scented.

We have a rose garden growing on the side of the hill. I will never forget the thrill of having two roses named in my honour. I was given several bushes of each. One is named " Greer Garson," the other " Mrs. Miniver." The " Greer Garson " is a large pink rose, and has a healthy look. " Mrs. Miniver " is a bright red, a colour that expresses the gaiety of Jan Struther's unforgettable character. I was really humble when I saw the bushes in full bloom. Because of the honour paid to me by their growers I have a feeling that these roses are " family."

I have talked so much about my own garden, now let me take you, in imagination, to some of the other lovely gardens I have found in California. Atwater Kent, well-known philanthropist and host at some of Hollywood's most interesting parties, has magnificent gardens surrounding his hilltop home in Bel Air. One formal garden on his extensive grounds has 300 steps flanked with trimmed cypress trees. There are whole beds of rare and exotic bird-of-paradise plants, a semi-tropical bloom of brilliant orange and deep blue from which nature has fashioned a flower which looks just like a bird in flight. Mr. Kent also has a garden with every known kind of desert flower.

At the studio the between-scene talk on the set often turns to gardens. Van Heflin's pride is his collection of roses, while Rosalind Russell grows hydrangea and Gladys Cooper used to discuss everything from zinnias to strawberry barrels when there was time for a chat on the set of " Mrs. Parkington." Strawberry barrels are not new to Britishers but in California they are a novelty. Gladys painted hers white and they stood quite high beside the steps leading from her front porch to the lower garden. At tea time the guests could pick all the strawberries the birds had overlooked. Gladys told me she was quite certain the birds thought the barrels were there just for their benefit !

Sir Aubrey and Lady Smith live on a delightful hilltop. A lovely lawn sweeps around their house but during the war it was dug up and planted with vegetables. Now, however, the lawn is back, and Lady Smith takes great pride in the flowers bordering it.

California is filled with brave souls who plant lawns in spite of the fact they are a great responsibility. Because of the long, rainless summer they need constant watering, fertilizing and sowing. Practically every humble cottage, as well as the more pretentious homes, has a broad lawn between the house and the street.

Most homes have " yards " in the back, usually surrounded by hedges, thick clumps of banana trees or may be a vine-covered wall to give the privacy lacking in the front. Often these " back yards " have badminton courts, space for table tennis or a barbecue. In the days when Mexico ruled California, I am told that a barbecue was a deep pit in the ground in which the whole carcass of a pig, lamb or steer was roasted by placing embers beneath and on top. Modern barbecues are more like an outdoor brick oven with an open grill of iron or steel on top, or maybe a revolving spit, where chops, steaks and chicken are broiled over charcoal.

The rows of towering, thin-trunked palm trees which stand like graceful sentinels on so many residential streets were a constant source of wonderment to me until, one day, I saw a row of trees which looked positively aflame. I found they were flowering eucalyptus —or what the "Aussies" term "flowering gums." But no sooner had the wonderment of these flamboyant trees passed when spring brought another surprise. This time it was the jacaranda trees which burst forth from winter hibernation with a solid mass of purplish, bluish bell-shaped blossoms that inspire poets to burst into verse. Imagine a tree as large as a well-grown oak becoming one mass of sapphire-like colouring! When the blossoms drop, feathery green foliage takes their place.

I am told the old settlers used the thorny, spine-covered cactus as a protection against robbers. Outside a window it is as effective as the staunchest iron bars. Only a suit of armour would offer protection from its porcupine-like thorns. There are many kinds of cactus in as many sizes and shapes, though it is almost always green. Some types blossom with pink, yellow and red flowers during the spring season.

Boris Karloff and Eve Arden are among the stars who live in hillside homes but use creeping vines to bind the soil instead of costly terraces and stone walls. Where houses cling to hillsides around Hollywood, Beverley Hills and Santa Monica, plants are invaluable in preventing erosion. Though it seldom rains in Southern California, when it does rain it pours. English ivy, wild strawberries and various succulents are used to prevent slides and make the slopes beautifully green.

Even film actresses get fun out of sweeping up the leaves—a constant job at Greer Garson's Bel Air home, because of the huge sycamores that tower above her lovely garden. Gogo, the French poodle, will have none of it.

No story of California and its gardens would be complete without some reference to the mission gardens. Most of the restored missions have replanted the gardens as they were in the days when the Franciscan fathers founded the outposts of civilization in the then wilderness of California. Many are now in ruins but some have been rebuilt. And today, as in the time of their Spanish founders, matilija poppies, Castilian roses, bougainvillea vines, olive trees, Catalina cherries and Seville oranges blend with the white-plastered adobe walls and sunburned red-tiled roofs of these historic old buildings. There are many more elaborate gardens in this golden state, but in the shadows of the stately bell towers and graceful archways of the old missions we find the first gardens of California.

I was staked

I WAS one of the thousands who hitch-hiked to California, hoping to crash the movies. All I crashed was an oil station—after drawing a zero for efforts to land a singing or acting job.

There was always accounting. I had had a good job with the Gulf Oil Company, but somehow I rebelled at taking on a job that meant eight hours a day perched on a stool—the California climate made you feel you wanted to be out in it. So I took a job pumping gas at a filling station in the San Fernando Valley.

I'll never forget the day, warm and vibrant. A fellow felt good. I was singing as I worked. The owner of the station came in to check the business. " Hello, young man. That's some voice—what are you doing working around here ? " I told him that others did not share his opinion of my voice. After all, I had to earn a living—the movies didn't want me ; I couldn't even get a night-club job, so here I was.

Perhaps a little study might be the thing. He was looking me over as he talked, as if summing me up. " It might," I said, " but it takes money." " Of course it does. I'm aware of that, but I would like to stake you to some lessons, and I'll give you fifty dollars a week to live on, say, for six months." He waited for my answer. I was speechless. It was not usual for such an offer to be made, literally out of the blue. " Later on when you have made the grade you can pay me twenty-five per cent of your salary until you have paid me back." And he waited for me to say something. I managed to blurt out, " I'll take it on." I started to study and worked hard, but the six months stretched out into two years. When I felt my voice was ready, I sang for an agent. After listening to me sing, he said, " Can you act ? " Hmm, does that mean he thinks I might have a better chance as an actor than a singer ? I told him no. He said, " Why not go the Pasadena Playhouse, get some acting experience ? " I took his advice, and my backer, the gas station owner, went right along providing the wherewithal. His belief in me helped me believe in myself. One night a Goldwyn talent scout saw me, arranged a test, and I signed a contract with Mr. Goldwyn. That was an exciting and hopeful moment. But he was not producing anything at the time. " Stay on at the Playhouse," I was advised. I began to get some attention from the critics.

Left : When Making " Canyon Passage " Dana Andrews had to help his wife over some of the wild streams in the rugged country of Oregon, where the film was made.

Right : Dana Andrews likes tinkering with toys, which are Christmas presents for children of his friends.

140

to a career

A tense moment at the divorce trial in 20th Century-Fox's forthcoming " Daisy Kenyon." Nicholas Joy and Ruth Warwick face up to Joan Crawford and Dana Andrews.

They praised my performance as George Washington in " Valley Forge." At last the day came when I was asked to report to the studio. It was for a small part in " The Westerner," with Gary Cooper, but I was excited at the prospect of getting before the camera.

In the meantime I had fallen in love with Mary Todd. She was an actress, but she was willing to give up her own career to play the role of Mrs. Andrews. At the time we thought we ought to wait for Mr. Goldwyn to give his consent to our marriage. What did Mr. Goldwyn have to do with it? you ask. A lot. I had been advised by another executive that I should not marry until I had become established—some sort of an idea that marriage did not foster the romantic appeal of young actors. I was advised to be " seen " at glamour spots with young glamour girls. But I still concentrated all my attention on Mary, so at the end of six months, this executive threw up his hands and told me to ask Mr. Goldwyn if I could marry the girl. I chased him for six weeks, but he had things far more important to him on his mind. At last I got him to listen to me and he said to go ahead. By that time I had a nice stubble of beard. I had to grow it for my part in " The Westerner "—and then I was really embarrassed. Would Mary want to marry me looking as I did? No girl can possibly think there is any romance to a man with a three weeks' growth of beard, I thought. But Mary married me, beard and all. She is a wonderful wife. Thanks to her family book-keeping and determined budgeting we managed to pay off in full my debt to the man who had taken a chance and put cash straight down the dotted line. A few weeks after we had made the last payment he died. I felt the world had lost a wonderful man and I a very real friend. My sadness, however, was tempered by the satisfaction of having repaid him —not that he needed the money, but he did need the assurance of believing in his ability to judge men. I was not the only young chap he had helped. He was always backing someone or doing some fine humanitarian deed. Several years before he died he helped a crippled fellow get his health back.

141

by DANA ANDREWS

He sent him to a bone specialist, footed the bills and then, when he was well, set him up in business. The man did well and I believe succeeded in meeting his indebtedness—but if either of us had not succeeded there would have been nothing said. He was that kind of fellow. He believed in investing in human beings.

My career grew. 20th Century-Fox asked to share my contract. My family grew, too—Mary and I have three children and I have a son by my first wife, who died. I shall never forget the happiness I felt over the way Mary took my five-year old son to her heart when we married. She became his " mother." The word " stepmother " was never used or thought of.

It is only recently we have been able to afford some of the things we have wanted but could not have because we had to repay—and how gladly—my friend. Now we have a home of our own and, for week-end relaxation, a 45-foot boat.

The first good holiday I have I am going for a South Sea island cruise, but the way parts are lining up it will be very much in the future. In the meantime, a fishing trip to Mexican waters is about all I get time for—and, of course, each Sunday we go down to Wilmington where we keep the " Katharine " (named after our daughter) tied up.

Whenever we go fishing I recall an incident that happened when I was a boy back in Texas and Dad and I went fishing. I was at home from school with a cold. Dad, who was a minister, wanted to go fishing and asked me if I felt well enough to go . . . of course I did. A cold might keep me away from school but never from a day's fishing. Off we went. Dad pulled beauties out of the river all day long and I never had a nibble. I was feeling pretty low. Just as we were leaving to go home I said, " I'll show you ! " and threw my line over a rocky ledge. I was incredulous when, the moment the hook hit the water, there was a tug—a big one. I fought that fish for half an hour. Dad would not give me a helping hand—he knew it would make me much happier to land him alone. I did. It was a twenty-pound catfish—the biggest of the day. Dad put his arm around me and said, " Son, you're the champion fisherman of the family." Dad is gone now, but I always think of him every time I go fishing.

Left : For week-end relaxation, Dana Andrews has a 45-ft. yacht. The studios keep him so busy, he has only time for fishing trips to Mexican waters, but he plans a South Sea island cruise.

Right : Two of the screen's most attractive personalities star in 20th Century-Fox's " Daisy Kenyon." Dana Andrews has Joan Crawford for his leading lady, and Henry Fonda will also be seen in the cast.

THANKS to my DANCING
by BETTY GRABLE

MY love for horses goes back to the days when I was a very small girl in the bustling mid western city of St. Louis. Horses were to me what dolls are to most small girls. Next to them, I liked dancing best. However, dancing meant lessons, while riding was sheer joy.

When the subject of lessons came up, I invariably thought it would be more fun to be out playing, until Mother would say, " Betty, do you want to go riding Saturday ? " I knew what that meant : No lessons, no riding. That was all I needed to make me practise. I danced and danced until every step was perfect—that weekly ride meant so much to me.

Later, when our family moved to Hollywood from St. Louis, where I was born, it was dancing that got me my first break in films. I danced and danced for a solid year as a member of the Fox chorus when the studio was at Western and Sunset. From then on everything I did seemed to boost me a step up the movie ladder. Very seldom did I have time for a good gallop—and never the chance to ride in shows as I had in my school days, winning highly prized cups. No, horses had to be forgotten in the crowded days that seem part of every actress's life, once she starts in earnest on a career. So time passed.

Life was very full—I was happy—I had travelled all over the country with top name bands which always seemed to bring me to the attention of the studios. In my career, being absent from Hollywood always helped me to land into better spots each time. Playing in " Du Barry was a Lady " on Broadway led to my present contract with 20th Century-Fox. When Alice Faye had the bad luck to become very ill before " Down Argentine Way " was started, I was asked to play her part. All this was very good— I liked to work—I was proud to be succeeding, but I had had to forget all about horses and riding, except on very rare occasions.

Time pranced on. I married band-leader Harry James. He came from Texas— he yearned for a ranch and, above all, he loved horses. So one bright day I walked out of the door of our Coldwater Canyon house and there stood two perfectly beautiful horses. I was so excited. So was Harry—so were the horses when they had to live in close quarters. It just wasn't fair . . . Harry and I went shopping for a ranch. At last we found a place we and the horses would like : sixty-three acres, with two little houses already built on it, were for sale. So we bought the Baby J Ranch, as we named it.

In the saddle are Harry James and daughter Vicki. Obviously keeping a careful eye on both is wife and mother Betty Grable.

It lies on the outskirts of a tiny little town, Calabasas—thirty miles from where the stagecoaches halted in the old days at the general store, which is still standing; and further up the road is the Court where, not so long ago, they tried horse and cattle thieves who raided the cattle ranches along the highway; and there is the Hangman's Tree where they were strung up; and also the famous adobe ranch house of the Agoura family stands, a monument to the days when the sixty-three acres were undoubtedly a part of the Agoura Rancho. There were fields green with corn—others well grassed for grazing, and twenty steel wire-fenced exercise pens for the racing and riding stock—the stables and operational buildings all clean and white.

Our two horses—I named mine Sugar, Harry called his Trumpet—kicked up their heels in approval when we brought them to their new home. "This is the life" they seemed to whinny. I knew just how they felt. Harry and I metaphorically kicked up our heels and proceeded to buy more horses, brood mares, fillies and colts, and eventually a stable of twelve racehorses.

We had a lot of fun fixing up the ranch house and the small caretaker's house close to the gate. I did most of the decorating myself. I used to go shopping for curtains, rugs, and the sort of things a country house needs.

The colour scheme is white and red. The living room floor is covered with a white string rug. I can hear you saying, "A white rug in a country house?—doesn't it get dirty too quickly?" If it does, it is the kind that can be washed and it is made in sections

One of the last films to come from the master hand of the late Ernst Lubitsch is 20th Century-Fox's "That Lady in Ermine." Betty Grable appears to be in a dispute between her two handsome leading men, Cesar Romero (left) and Douglas Fairbanks Jnr.

so it is easily tubbed. I slipcovered the chairs in a red and white patterned sturdy chintz. The old-fashioned oil lamps have a cherry border around their antique glass shades. They give a cheerful light—but, of course, they are wired for electricity. In front of the calico-covered couch stands an old cobbler's bench—I found it in an antique shop and decided it was just the thing for a coffee table.

The kitchen . . . ah, that is really our pride and joy. We think almost as much of that as we do of our stables. I put linoleum on the floor, and we have a porcelain stove and a refrigerator. Both were hard to find, for there are still shortages in these items. I shopped for the curtains—they had to be a certain size—but I eventually found what I wanted.

We sleep in true ranch style. Our bedroom has two double-tiered bunks.

But the pride and joy of the Baby J are the stables and our horses. Even Vicki, now four, has a special interest in them. Her runabout buggy—a gift from the members of her daddy's band—with shiny wheels is drawn by a gentle young mare we call "Colleen." Vicki always sits up straight as an arrow and she knows how to hold the reins properly. She rides too, sometimes with her daddy and sometimes on her own pony. One of my fans sent Vicki a pair of beautifully-made cowboy boots.

We are really proud of our hand-tooled black saddles. Harry chose them, seeing he is an old Texas rancher. While I could always ride, Harry is teaching me all there is to know about running the stables. Our horses mean so much to us that we have both arranged our contracts so they give us free time each year to take our children and spend the racing season at Del Mar. There I am so happy with my family.

Star of this picture, Betty Grable would say, is her horse "Sugar." Betty's greatest hobby in life is horse-riding.

Naturally, I have my favourite among the horses, "Red Ear" is his name. He has the nicest brown face and a white spot on his nose. I always rub that white spot and tell him it's for luck. When our last baby decided to arrive prematurely, I 'phoned Harry, who was in the East, and asked him to please go down to where our horses were then stabled and rub "Red Ear's" white spot. He did not laugh or say anything about my making such a request. He said, "Of course, dear"—and, "We will know everything will be all right." With Harry's reassurances to buoy me up, I went off to the hospital. I was quite ill, but little Jessica arrived safely and we were very happy. She is, according to her sister Vicki, "beautiful."

When she can get away from the pressure of work at the studios, Betty is happiest taking a morning canter with husband Harry James round their Baby J Ranch.

After I was well enough and "Red Ear" was back in his own stables, I had a grateful heart-to-heart talk with him.

We expect the future to bring lots of improvements at the Baby J. "Pop," my father, takes care of it for us when we are in town. Harry has to be away a lot and I have to stay in town all week when I'm making a picture.

As I look around the place and pay the horses a visit, I wonder if this would have all been possible if I had not danced my feet off to get that precious Saturday morning ride on a hired horse.

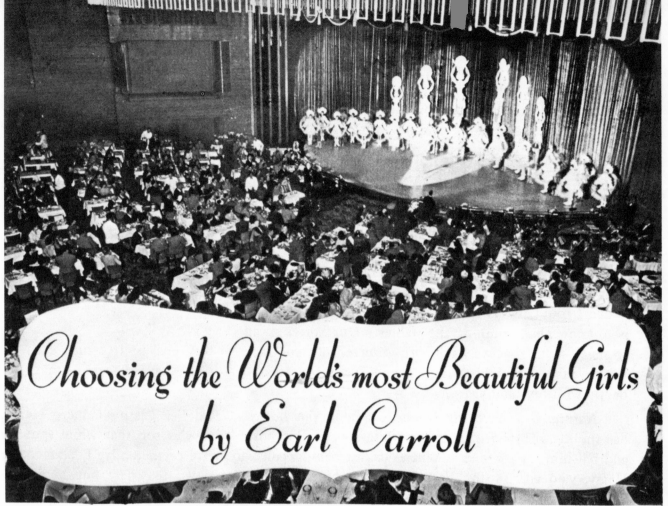

Choosing the World's most Beautiful Girls
by Earl Carroll

The huge revolving stages of Earl Carroll's theatre-restaurant serve as a dance floor between shows.

"THROUGH these portals pass the most beautiful girls in the world."
I coined this phrase many seasons ago during the run of one of my New York revues. I had it printed and hung above the stage door of the theatre where we were playing. Through the years, on the stage doors of theatres all over the country and now in Hollywood, the slogan has remained with me. I like to think of it as my way of showing appreciation to all the lovely young girls who have contributed so much to my work in the theatre. Without them, mine might have been a vastly different career.

As a boy I never entertained notions of any career but one in the theatre. It had been my life ever since I was old enough to get a job as a programme boy. Later as I worked at various jobs such as stage manager and box office manager I began to be curious about the field of production.

I decided that if I were to become a producer and a successful one I should know exactly what audiences liked best. I started to study audiences and to study the reaction of the public. I went from theatre to theatre. I visited all the cabarets and I paid particular attention to the work that was being done in the movies. And the longer I studied the more convinced I became of one outstanding factor—the importance of beauty in a theatrical presentation.

I soon realized that the most exciting thing one could put on a stage was a breathtakingly beautiful girl. She did not need to know how to dance or even to sing. All that was necessary was that she be beautiful. Yet in the face of an observation which a neophyte like myself had made in comparatively little time, few musical producers of that day seemed interested in presenting really beautiful girls in their shows.

I decided that I could and would. Thus, with the idea of the " beautiful girl " firmly implanted as the predominant factor I embarked on my first musical, " Earl Carroll's Vanities." I found my girls both inside and outside of the profession. There were no talent requirements—just some common sense and a great deal of beauty.

The girls more than fulfilled my greatest expectations and highest hopes. Our first " Vanities " was a hit from the start. For years thereafter I came back to Broadway with other editions and always the public proved my point ; they would rather see a beautiful girl doing nothing than an ugly person exhibiting the rarest talent in the world. Naturally this does not apply to all fields in the theatre but it is a vital factor in musicals.

Ten years ago in Hollywood I opened a theatre-restaurant—a daring experiment in a city of unpredictable night club habits. It was a costly venture for in its construction I fulfilled all my dreams of a perfect theatre. It features a huge, double revolving stage measuring 225 feet. There are pillars which can be turned into circular staircases and side boxes which appear magically from draped walls.

Nothing so lavish had been attempted before in Hollywood or, for that matter, else-where in the world. However apprehensive I may have felt at the wisdom of spending so much money on a theatre, I still had faith in my theory of beautiful girls. And just as they had accounted for the success of the " Vanities " in New York, the girls did the same in the west. A highly satisfactory tourist season saved our theatre from going to the wall. People who were visiting California from other parts of the country long had heard of the " Carroll girls " or, perhaps, had seen them in New York. They came to see them again and we were on our way to success—a success that has continued undiminished ever since.

Now the days of barnstorming the country are over ; gone is the excitement of preparing a show for Broadway, trying it out in the suburbs and then playing it a season or two on the road. The theatre-restaurant is pretty much a cut and dried business proposition and equally matter of fact is the continued search for beautiful girls. Perhaps I miss the days when Florenz Ziegfeld and myself fought over the contracts of famous showgirls. Perhaps I miss the excitement of opening night and the suspense of waiting for the newspaper reviews. But in these ten rather tranquil years I have been able to reach some interesting conclusions about my profession which is, after all, the presentation on the stage of beautiful girls.

To-day's show girl is quite different from her sister of a decade or so ago. She is much more independent, especially in the west, and she does not think of a tenure in the chorus as a career. There was a time when famous beauties would work on season after season without showing age and actually becoming more attractive as they matured.

The turnover is much greater than it used to be ; those with talent go on to the films and those less gifted soon settle down into quiet matrimony. Most of our girls come to us with no experience, yet we are able to train them within three or four weeks. They rapidly become accustomed to the routine of the theatre and they do not remain starry-eyed or entranced with the glamour of it for very long. They come to regard their two shows a night and an evening off as a routine not much different from a job in an office.

Discipline is strict and girls are forbidden to stay out late during the work week. They must be bright, alert and pretty for the evening performances. Nothing mars beauty quite so fast as late hours and habits injurious to health. Quite naturally, the girls sometimes resent this supervision of their personal lives and playing " possum " is a familiar tactic.

We have our particular technique for dealing with the girl who feigns illness in order to get a night off. The stage manager calls her house and keeps calling until he reaches her. If she is sick she is made to come to the phone and is given appropriate sympathy. If she " cannot " come to the telephone we let it be known that we draw our own conclusions and the girl understands that we comprehend all the tricks of playing hookey better than she.

Dealing with fifty or sixty young girls—all of whom are interested in normal fun and the excitement of having dates—gives one the same perspective and wily attitude as the headmistress of a boarding school. You have to be one jump ahead all the time.

That is why we always have a rehearsal on Tuesday afternoon whether we need one or not. Monday is the girls' free day and it is imperative that they are all back and ready for the Tuesday night show. You can imagine what a shambles would ensue if fifteen or twenty decided to stay out of town or remain sunning on the beach. The rehearsals allow for necessary replacements.

Another device that is used to make certain the girls care for themselves properly is my insistence that they wear up-sweep hair-dos. Personally I like that style better but over and above that preference, the rule insures proper grooming of the girls' hair. To wear it up requires at least a half hour of brushing and combing every day. And no one has discovered a better method of caring for hair than that.

There was a time when I lectured the girls on how to take care of their beauty and how to keep themselves beautiful. Regardless of what I said they did as they chose so now I find it simpler to make rules. Yet I cannot help but think what a pity it is that beautiful girls do not realize how priceless their beauty is.

It is a gift which should be looked upon with the same respect that is accorded any natural endowment. And beauty, I have learned, is not reserved for any particular group alone. Our girls come from every section of the United States and represent every social strata. We look for them in colleges, in shops and in other theatrical presentations. Regular calls are announced and aspirant show girls flock to the stage door.

They are assembled on the stage and then segregated according to height. Then, in lines of twenty, they step forward, count off, make quarter turns and face forward. Those who measure up to our standards are asked to step out and give their names and addresses to the stage manager. This schedule is repeated until only one hundred or so remain. To this number are added the lovely girls selected in subsequent calls.

After the group has been narrowed down to some 300 girls, each is given a brief personal interview. The following points of beauty are given careful consideration: colour and texture of hair, brilliancy and s i z e o f e y e s, r e g u l a r i t y of teeth, general colouring, texture of skin, f o r m a t i o n o f hands and feet, posture and (very i m p o r t a n t) personality.

With final selections made, the chosen few are ready for rehearsal.

Can you spot the signature of your favourite movie star? It will probably be amongst the autographs which cover the wall of Earl Carroll's famous theatre-restaurant in Hollywood.

It is not an easy job and not always successful. There are times (and this was particularly true during the war) when it was necessary to engage girls who do not have all the necessary qualifications. We replace them when it is possible.

Still this does not reflect completely on the girls themselves, for beauty, we must remember, is relative. A girl can be obscured in our show because she is surrounded by so much beauty yet it is possible for her to hold her own on another theatre platform.

Often I am asked for the ideal Earl Carroll Girl's specifications. Here they are and if any of you English beauties happen to fill them and happen to be out Hollywood way, perhaps you will drop in to see me.

EARL CARROLL'S IDEAL GIRL

Height	5 ft. 5½ in.	Hips	35½ in.
Weight	8 st. 8 lbs.	Thigh	19½ in.
Neck	12 in.	Ankle	9 in.
Bust	34½ in.	Wrist	6 in.

Waist 24 in.

Readers of "Hollywood Album" will share our regret that while this article was at press, Earl Carroll and Beryl Wallace were killed in an air-crash.—The Publishers.

Van Heflin, Ward Bond and Richard Long star in Universal-International's " Tap Roots."

Betty Hutton plays several parts in Paramount's " Dream Girl."

Bob Hope will co-star with Jane Russell in Paramount's " The Pale Face."

Rosalind Russell has Raymond Massey (above), Michael Redgrave, Leo Genn and Kirk Douglas as co-stars in R.K.O.'s " Mourning Becomes Electra."

Melvyn Douglas, Cary Grant and Myrna Loy in R.K.O.'s " Mr. Blandings builds his Dream House."

John Lund, Gail Russell and Edward G. Robinson in Paramount's " Night has a Thousand Eyes."

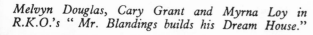

Ronald Colman in Universal-
International's " Double Life."

Myrna Loy, Louis Calhern, Robert Mitchum
and (right) Shepperd Strudwick in Republic's
" The Red Pony."

Orson Welles in his own production of " Macbeth."

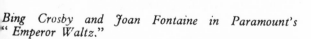

Bing Crosby and Joan Fontaine in Paramount's
" Emperor Waltz."

Harold Lloyd in " Mad Wednesday," a Preston
Sturges comedy.

David O. Selznick's "The Paradine Case." In the
dock is new star Valli. Her defence counsel (left) is
Gregory Peck. Bottom right is Charles Coburn.

Joan Crawford

CHILDREN are important to most women—very few can truthfully say they are not. I am very humble, very grateful that I have been able to adopt and am able to provide well for four children. Perhaps there will be more added to my family.

Some people have wondered at my plunging into the responsibility of bringing up one boy and three girls, and I will admit it is a responsibility, but a self-sought one : they are all adopted.

I started with Christina ; she is eight, a sensitive child with very blue eyes and very blonde hair. She is a very serious child, thinks a lot, has a decided will of her own. It is not easy to discipline her, but I am forced to when she insists on doing things her own way. I find punishing her by hurting her dignity is very effective. She is the eldest of the family and likes to feel she is looked up to especially by Christopher. And when she behaves well she is ; so when she deliberately disobeys a specific order I have given her, I send her to bed before Christopher. She is crushed because she feels she has lost face in his estimation.

Her brother Christopher is a chubby, cuddly boy of five—always laughing, and has a way with him that makes it hard not to spoil him. But that is one thing I am determined not to do. It is much harder to make him do things for himself than do them for him, but I insist he dresses himself, picks up his clothes and keeps his toys neatly. Happy-go-lucky Christopher would much rather leave things behind and coax everyone to wait on him. His little conscience is very clear; he sleeps with a smile, such a contented smile.

Meet My Children

The two youngest are so young—they are just babies: Cynthia is ten months and Cathy eight. But they have their own definite personalities. Cynthia (we call her Cindy) is all energy, kicking her little feet so gaily and always making an effort to stand and walk. I think she will be a dancer; she makes such definite motions. Cathy is a quiet little thing. She lies peacefully in her crib and looks and looks . . . I often wonder what babies see, very little I am told, but they get such a faraway look, you think perhaps they are seeing all sorts of wonderful things.

When I look ahead, then I visualize a life that will have great interest for me, the unfolding of the four characters; in bringing them up it will help me discipline myself.

I have taken them on of my own free will and I must give them a fair deal all the way through. They give me intense happiness now in their early childhood, but later on they will be exerting their own individualities; then I will certainly be put on my mettle. I am not unaware of situations that can and will come up; but I pray—oh, so very hard— that I will be equal to them. I am fortunate in having an excellent governess to help care for them. She is watching their manners. I get quite a thrill when I come in for dinner—I have formed the habit of eating with them—and there they are, Christina and Christopher, standing by their chairs. Five-thirty is an early hour for me, but when I am working it is impossible to see them as much as I would like, so I always have dinner at their hour when I can.

Joan Crawford has four adopted children, the two eldest of whom are Christopher (left) and Christina.

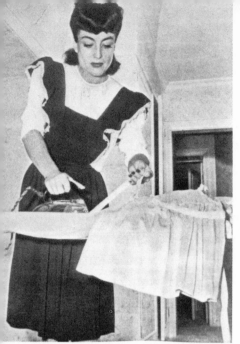

Little girls' clothes must be washed and ironed, and lovely Joan Crawford is quite capable of doing up her daughter Christina's clothes.

Since the children came the house has been enlarged so they can have plenty of room. There is a swimming pool where we have fun and a lot of healthy exercise. They have a garden to play in, and go for walks in the neighbourhood. It is still rather like the country in Brentwood, nice paths for walking and lots of flowers and trees. Christina goes to a local school and gets along very well. Her favourite hobbies are riding horses and her dancing lessons.

Christopher just wants to be a cowboy and have guns and horses.

I dress them simply—although Christina has some lovely party dresses. I remember how I always wanted pretty dresses when I was her age, so I see she has them, but not too many to spoil her !

It is one of my theories that everyone should try to get away—completely away from Hollywood each year. So I started on a trip to Hawaii. Everything was well planned, the children had their nurse and well-tried servants to take care of them ; goodbyes were said ; the children came to see me off ; we were all decorated with flowers— presents galore greeted me in the cabin stateroom. It was all very " gala "—I was really going to have a wonderful holiday in the land of the luaua and surfboard. The trip across was wonderful. I spent lazy days doing absolutely nothing, then came the excitement of landing at Honolulu. The natives swam out to meet the boat, we all threw coins for them to dive for, the band played, lovely soft voices sang their plaintive songs, the scent of flowers was in the air, the day was perfect.

I walked gaily down the gangplank and was whisked away to the hotel. I had no sooner unpacked, than something happened. I was engulfed in a wave of homesickness. " Let's go home," I said to my secretary, Thea Larsen—I had brought her along for company and because she needed a holiday, too. She is a most faithful Girl Friday. She looked at me a little bewildered, but she knows me so well she understood—so back we came. People could not believe it, but it happened. No one was sick, nothing was wrong, it was just I, who hurried back to the laughter and chatter of Christina and Christopher. Foolish perhaps, but that's what my self-enforced role of motherhood means to me.

Joan Crawford's children, Christopher (left) and Christina (right), accompany their mother as she goes to the docks to take off for a holiday in Honolulu. Miss Crawford returned after a 24 hour stay in the Hawaiian Islands—she got homesick for her children.

Out of  the Hat
Peter Godfrey

EARLY in 1914 a fit-up company was travelling in Ireland and decided they wanted a new utility boy—that is, somebody to play anything that nobody else would play. I answered the advertisement and joined the company immediately afterwards, having received my fare from the manager. I had no idea what a fit-up company was until I joined them in a little town called Enniskillen. These small theatrical companies toured the countryside, erecting their own proscenium arches and scenery in local halls or even tents. I found that the actors not only played their parts on the stage, but also sold the tickets, showed people to their seats, and worked as stage hands. The biggest shock was when the manager said to me, " What sort of an act do you do ? ", and I found out that between the scenes of the play I was expected to do some sort of a turn. It was then I thought of my hobby, which happened to be magic. So I made my first professional appearance as a magician in between the scenes of a melodrama called " Shall We Forgive Her ? "

Magic had been my hobby since the age of ten, when I saw Horace Goldin vanish a tiger at the " Woolwich Hippodrome." I nearly made my first appearance as a magician at the age of eleven. It was a Speech Day concert at my school. For a whole year I had spent my pocket money in buying tricks for this show, and every one was made of glass—a tumbler, a casket, a lamp chimney, etc.—for I was to be billed as " The *Crystal* Magician." On the night of the performance I made my entrance. Two boys were to lift my table and apparatus onto the stage. I started my opening speech : " Ladies and gentlemen, with your kind permission for a few minutes I shall have much pleasure in presenting a few tricks of magic." At this point there was a terrifying crash offstage. In getting the table up the stairs, the boys had tipped it, and all my tricks had slipped off and were smashed on the floor. I stood in the middle of the stage, crying, until they hauled me off.

But in spite of this heart-breaking beginning, I still have magic as my hobby, and in between writing, directing and acting in plays and films I have found time to make one or two professional appearances. For thirteen months I was the Magical Master of Ceremonies at the London Pavilion in Piccadilly Circus and played two engagements at Maskelyne's Mysteries. After I arrived in Hollywood, I found I had very little time for anything but my work in films until the war broke out, and then I revived the act

and did over a thousand shows for the troops in camps, hospitals, etc.

I consider magic the finest hobby a boy can have. I have always found it a great help in my work on the stage and in films, especially as an actor. The co-ordination of hand and eye, which magic teaches, is a great help to the actor. In directing, timing is of primary importance, and this can be learned from magic more quickly and easily than from any other means I know.

Entertainment has not been the only use to which magic may be put. In 1853 the French Emperor Napoleon III appointed Jean Antoine Houdin, one of the most famous of all magicians, as a special imperial envoy to Algeria. The Arabs were threatening to revolt at a time most inopportune for France. Politicians criticized Napoleon for his appointment of a trickster for the delicate mission of maintaining peace in Africa, but Napoleon and Houdin had a few tricks up their sleeves which they kept to themselves.

Houdin's mission was to impress the Arabs with the fact that a revolt would be futile in face of the might of France. Until Houdin's arrival, however, the Arabs figured France was too weakened by other wars to put up much of a fight. Houdin entertained the Bey and his advisers at a lavish banquet. He said that he would amuse them with a few feats of magic.

Houdin produced a small chest which was easily carried into the banquet hall by two servants. He invited the Arabs to test their strength and lift the chest from the floor. The Arabs laughed, for the chest was as light as a feather and none of the banqueters had trouble lifting it single-handed. " Now," said Houdin, " I will invoke my powers and make each of you so weak that not even all of you together can lift the chest." The Arabs scoffed. But when they tried to move it the chest would not budge. Beads of perspiration stood out on their foreheads as the Bey and six of his advisers strained and tugged to no avail.

Houdin smiled. When the Arabs had given up he went over and picked up the chest with a single hand. The Arabs, fearing Houdin's mysterious power to make strong men weak, signed a treaty promising not to make war on France. Only Napoleon III and Houdin knew the secret of this " mysterious power." You see, Houdin was the inventor of the electric magnet. Thus a magician and a simple trick of legerdemain saved France's vast colonial empire in North Africa. Maybe some of our contemporary statesmen might well learn a few tricks, too !

As you may know, in every country in the world there are societies of magicians banded together for their mutual help. When I was in England I was a member of the Inner Magic Circle, which boasts over a thousand members. When I came to America, the first people to contact me on my arrival in New York were members of the American Society of Magicians, founded many years ago by Harry Houdini. Again, when I stepped off the plane in Hollywood, I was greeted by magicians belonging to Los Magicos, the leading magic group in California. My English friends will no doubt be surprised to hear that there are five magic clubs in Hollywood, with membership of about five hundred active magicians. Once a year I organize these magicians and we give a show here in Hollywood for the stars and their children.

There are many rabid magic fans in the film world : Chester Morris, Orson Welles, Ronald Colman, Harold Lloyd, Jimmy Stewart, Warner Baxter, Henry Fonda and Edgar Bergen, to mention a few. They all find it a great help in their work, as I have done. Whenever you see these stars doing magic in a film, you will know that it is the real thing and not camera magic. When we were making " The Woman in White," which stars Sidney Greenstreet, Alexis Smith and Eleanor Parker, I found that everyone needed cheering up. I did a few silk tricks and pulled rabbits out of my hat, poured water in seemingly never-ending quantities from a flower vase, and had not only Alexis' and Eleanor's bewilderment for my reward, but found that Sidney Greenstreet himself accepted me as his master in the art of black magic. In my present picture, " The Decision of Christopher Blake," I myself could not resist the exhibitionist in me. You will, if the fascinating performances of the stars permit you to notice me and my wife Renee in the picture, see me do a little trick with Ted Donaldson's hair. In this particular case I shall give away my secret : I did it with fine white thread. But otherwise I am in no position to give any clues as to how tricks are done. As a member of the various associations of magicians, I am pledged to secrecy.

" Peterkin Does It Again "— Chester Morris, Columbia star of the Boston Blackie series, magician-par-excellence, plays stooge to Gerrie Larsen's hand-operated rabbit, Peterkin, as he selects a card chosen by Jeff Donnell. Bill Larsen, who operates a Hollywood shop devoted to magicians' supplies, looks on.

ACKNOWLEDGEMENTS

OUR SINCERE APPRECIATION TO THE FOLLOWING COMPANIES AND MEMBERS OF THEIR ORGANIZATIONS FOR THE CO-OPERATION WHICH MADE *HOLLYWOOD ALBUM* POSSIBLE.

COLUMBIA PICTURES CORPORATION

Ely Levy—Head of Studio International Department, Hollywood
Viola MacDonald-Moore
Alan E. Tucker (London)

WALT DISNEY PRODUCTIONS

Joseph Reddy—Director Studio Publicity
Gil Souto—Studio Foreign Publicity
Jack Jungmeyer

METRO-GOLDWYN-MAYER STUDIOS

Howard Strickling—Director Studio Publicity
Robert Vogel—Head of Studio International Department
Edward Lawrence
Richard Morean
Dorothy Blanchard
Clarence Bull and Eric Carpenter for colour photography
Frank Fowell (London)

MONOGRAM PICTURES CORPORATION

Louis S. Lifton   Director Studio Publicity

REPUBLIC PRODUCTIONS, INC.

Mort Goodman—Director Studio Publicity
Bill Rogers—Studio International Department
Roman Freulich—colour photography

R.K.O. RADIO PICTURES, INC.

Adele Palmer—Studio Foreign Department
William Hebert—Director of Publicity for Samuel Goldwyn
Alfred A. Vaughn—Director of Publicity for Sierra Productions
David Jones (London)

VANGUARD FILMS INC.

(Selznick International Pictures)

Paul MacNamara—vice-president in charge of public relations
Hyatt Daab—in charge of foreign press
Paul G. Smith Jr.
Joan Lane
John Michle—photography

UNIVERSAL-INTERNATIONAL STUDIOS

Louis Blaine—Director Studio Foreign Publicity
Ray Jones—colour photography
Jack Sullivan (London)

20th CENTURY-FOX FILM CORPORATION

W. M. (Doc) Bishop—Director, Studio International Department
Roy Metzler
Frank Powolony—colour photography
Selby Howe (London)

WARNER BROS.—FIRST NATIONAL PICTURES

Carl Schaefer—Manager, Studio International Department
Walter Klinger
Carl Combs
Jerry Kauffman
Bert Six, Floyd McCarty, Fred Morgan, Eugene Riches—colour photography
Ernest Player (London)

PARAMOUNT PICTURES

Edward Schellhorn—Director Studio Foreign Publicity
Arlene DuBois
Walter Seltzer, Hal Wallis Productions
" Whitey " Schafer—colour photography
Marjorie Booth (London)

UNITED ARTISTS

Lincoln Quarberg—Director of Publicity for Howard Hughes Productions
Gaston Valcourt

ENTERPRISE STUDIOS

William F. Blowitz   Director of Publicity

* * *

Lyle Rooks of Henry Rogers Company
Helen Ferguson
Jewel Smith
Jean Pettebone—Bob Wachsman
Lida Livingstone, Paul Marsh and William Walsh of Margaret Ettinger and Company
Ruth Winner of Earl Carroll's Theatre-Restaurant
Bev Barnett
Helen Blanke of the House of Westmore
Emil Cuhel for special photographs

P. H. Powell, New York Correspondent of the London *Star*, for his invaluable assistance at all times